On the Saints
SERMONS BY SAINT GREGORY PALAMAS

ON THE SAINTS
Sermons by Saint Gregory Palamas

edited by
Christopher Veniamin

MOUNT THABOR PUBLISHING
2008

First edition 2008

Mount Thabor Publishing
184 Saint Tikhon's Road
Waymart, PA 18472-4521 USA

www.thaborian.com

Printed in the United States of America

Library of Congress Cataloging-in-Publication Data

Gregory Palamas, Saint, 1296-1359.
[Sermons. Selections. English]
On the saints : sermons by Saint Gregory Palamas / edited by Christopher Veniamin. -- 1st ed.
p. cm. -- (Sermons by Saint Gregory Palamas ; v. 3)
ISBN 978-0-9774983-6-9
1. Christian saints--Sermons--Early works to 1800. 2. Orthodox Eastern Church--Sermons--Early works to 1800. I. Veniamin, Christopher, 1958- II. Title.
BX380.G7413 2008
252'.019--dc22

2008039638

Front cover:
Saint Demetrius. 16th century Byzantine Icon.
Photo Credit : Scala / Art Resource, NY
Benaki Museum, Athens, Greece

Archimandrite Sophrony
(1896 – 1993)
in memoriam aeternam

Saint Gregory Palamas
(1296–1359)
Chapel of the Holy Unmercenary Physicians
Vatopedi Monastery, Mount Athos

Luminary of the Orthodox faith,
support of the Church and teacher,
splendour of monastics,
invincible champion of theologians,
O wonderworker Gregory,
boast of Thessalonica,
preacher of grace,
pray without ceasing
that our souls be saved.

Dismissal Hymn (Apolytikion) of the Saint
Fourth Plagial (Tone Eight), Second Sunday in Great Lent

Contents

Foreword

ON THE SAINTS is the third volume in the series *Sermons by Saint Gregory Palamas,* the purpose of which is to bring the life and teaching of this remarkable fourteenth century saint (1296–1359) to a wider readership, to the layperson interested in the rich Biblical tradition of the Church Fathers.

Arranged thematically, the work in hand consists of seven sermons devoted to the Saints, including St. Gregory's wonderful homily on his fellow patron saint of Thessalonica, the Great Martyr Demetrius the Myrrhstreamer (3rd century), which is Homily 49 in the surviving corpus of sixty-three homilies. The other sermons in this edition, in liturgical sequence and with their corresponding numbers in the corpus, are on the Ancestors of God According to the Flesh (Homily 55), on the saints of the Old Testament (Homily 57), on St. John the Baptist (Homily 40), on SS. Peter and Paul (Homily 28), on St. John the Divine (Homily 44), and on All Saints (Homily 25).

It was in 1334, while on Mount Athos, in his third year at the hermitage of Saint Sabas, which belongs to the Great Lavra, that Palamas experienced a vision in which he was encouraged to share the wisdom bestowed upon him from on high. It seemed that he was carrying a vessel overflowing with milk, which subsequently turned into the finest of wines. The wine emitted such a strong fragrance that it brought great joy to his soul. A youth appeared and rebuked him for not sharing the wine with others and for allowing it to go to waste, for this wine, as he explained, was inexhaustible. The angel then warned Gregory, reminding him of the parable of the talents (*cf.* Matt. 25:14–30). As he later related to his friend and disciple Dorotheus,[1] Palamas understood this vision to mean that the time would come when he would be called upon to transfer his teaching from the simple plane of the ethical (the milk) to the higher plane of the dogmatic word (the wine), which leads heavenward.[2] Thus at the age of about thirty-eight Gregory began to write his Encomium for Saint Peter the Athonite, and, at about the same time, he also began to compose what is without doubt the most famous of all his works, Homily 53, "On the Entry of the Mother of God into the Holy of Holies", in which the *Theotokos* is presented as the archetype of the hesychastic way of life, the way of "stillness" (Gk. *hesychia, cf.* Ps. 46:10).

The teaching of Saint Gregory and his fellow Hesychasts was based on the understanding that man, the greatest of all God's creatures, had been called to enter into direct and unmediated communion with God even from this present life. The chief manner by which this is achieved is through the grace of God and *noetic* prayer, that is, through the Prayer of the Heart, also known as the Jesus Prayer: *Lord Jesus Christ, Son of God, have mercy upon me.* For the Hesychasts, therefore, true theology, real knowledge of God, is given not to those whose minds have been exercised in lofty concepts *about* God, but to those who, through prayer and ascetic striving in accordance with the commandments of Christ, have been made worthy to behold the vision of Christ in glory, to those who have seen God face to face and share in His very Life.

1. One of the Vlatte brothers (the other being Markos), who built Vlattadon Monastery (1351–1371). Dorotheus later also served as Archbishop of Thessalonica, from 1371 to 1379.

2. Philotheus Kokkinos, *Encomium for our father among the saints, Gregory Palamas, Archbishop of Thessalonica,* ed. J.-P. Migne, *Patrologia Graeca* 151:580A–581B; see esp. crit. ed. Demetrios G. Tsames, *The Hagiological Works of Philotheus Kokkinos, Patriarch of Constantinople,* vol. 1: *Thessalonian Saints,* Center for Byzantine Studies (Thessalonica, 1985), §§ 36–37, pp. 467–468.

Text and Translation

The present work is based on the edition of Panagiotes K. Chrestou.[3] The initial translation of the sermons contained in *On the Saints* was kindly made available to the editor for correction and improvement by Archimandrite Zacharias of the Holy Monastery of St. John the Baptist, England, and subsequently corrected against the original Greek, oftentimes reworked, and given its present form. Responsibility for the final version of the text, of course, rests entirely with the editor.

I wish to express my deepest gratitude to Abbot Ephraim and the brethren of the Holy Monastery of Vatopedi on Mount Athos for so kindly providing me with a copy of the oldest extant icon of St. Gregory: a 1371 wall-painting from the Chapel of the Holy Unmercenary Physicians (Gk. *Anargyroi*) at Vatopedi (see back cover and p. vi). The front cover icon is a 16th century depiction of St. Demetrius the Great Martyr and Myrrhstreamer.

A Note on Biblical References

Even though Saint Gregory himself used the Septuagint (Greek) text of the Old Testament, for purely practical reasons I have considered it expedient to employ the numbering, names, and wording of the Hebrew (Massoretic) text, as found in the more familiar Authorized (King James) Version. Scriptural quotations have been adjusted in favour of the Septuagint rendering only where significant differences occur. Such instances have been indicated by the use of LXX.

C. V.

SAINT TIKHON'S ORTHODOX THEOLOGICAL SEMINARY
FEAST *of* SAINT ANNA THE PROGENITOR OF GOD
9 SEPTEMBER, 2008

3. *Gregory Palamas: The Complete Works*, vols. 9–11, in the series *Greek Fathers of the Church*, nos. 72, 76, and 79 (Thessalonica, 1985–1986), with an accompanying Modern Greek rendering. This is the preliminary text for the critical edition by Professor Vasileios S. Pseutonkas, of the School of Theology in the University of Thessalonica, which is to occupy the sixth and final volume in Chrestou's *Gregory Palamas: Writings* (Thessalonica, 1962ff).

On the Ancestors of God According to the Flesh

When the only-begotten Son of God took flesh for us of the Virgin and, through His way of life in the flesh, fulfilled the law given by Moses (*cf.* Matt. 5:17, Rom. 10:4), perfected the law of grace and transformed that old law for our Church, the Hebrew race was expelled from the sacred Congregation and we were brought in instead, the elect from among the Gentiles, whom the Lord unites with Himself and the Father. He adopts us as true sons and brothers, and – Oh ineffable love for mankind! – even as His parents. "For whosoever", he says, "shall do the will of my Father which is in heaven, the same is my brother, and sister, and mother" (Matt. 12:50).

In church today, however, we celebrate the forefathers, most of whom were Hebrews by race. For what reason? So that all of us may learn that the Hebrews were not disinherited nor the Gentiles adopted as sons in a way that was unjust, unreasonable or unworthy of God who did these things and made these changes. Rather, just as among those Gentiles who were called, only the obedient were chosen for kinship with God, so the race of Israel, and Adam's descendants down to Israel's time, were a great multitude, but only those among them who lived according to God's will were true Israelites. To them the prophecies belonged, through them future events were prefigured, and to them the promises were given (*cf.* Rom. 3:1–4:13). Only these men were the true fathers and forefathers, firstly of her who in virginity bore Christ, who is God over all (Rom. 9:5), according to the flesh, and then, through Him, of ourselves. These fathers and forefathers were certainly not cast out of Christ's Church, for they are publicly commemorated by us today as partakers of the fullness of the saints. For in Christ Jesus there is neither old nor new, "nor Greek nor Jew, Barbarian, Scythian, bond nor free: but Christ is all and in all" (Col. 3:11, *cf.* Gal. 3:28). In Him there is no Jew, which is one merely outwardly, neither is there any circumcision, which is outward, but he is a Jew, which is one inwardly; and circumcision is that of the heart, in the spirit, and not in the letter of the law (Rom. 2:28–29). All, old and new, who have been well-pleasing to God, and all who have led lives acceptable to God, either before the law, under the law or after the law in the gospel of grace, have this circumcision and are united by it (*cf.* Rom. 4:10–12, Phil. 3:3, Col. 2:11).

If you look at God's dispensation for the human race with understanding, you will see that from beginning to end it is inwardly consistent and follows a logical order. It is now the case that the elect from every nation receive a new name as Christians, but those who are fruitless are rejected, "For many be called, but few chosen", as the Lord Himself says (Matt. 20:16). And it was the same with those who lived in ancient times and those of the Jewish nation who came after them. Of those people who received new names, only the elect were accepted, whereas the mass of unprofitable people among them were cast out. Of Seth's descendants, who were called the sons of God (*cf.* Gen. 6:2), those who were seized with mad desire for the daughters of men were, according to the Scripture, disinherited (*cf.* Gen. 6:3). The unprofitable majority among the Jews were not the proselytes, but those who were born Jewish, and were even legitimate sons, after the flesh, of Jacob, the first to bear the name of Israel (Gen. 32:28), yet were disobedient like Esau (*cf.* Gen. 26:34–35). Even Absalom, the son of the prophet and king David, their first ruler after Saul, was a stranger to the sacred race because he sought to kill his father (*cf.* 2 Sam. 16:8–11, 17:1ff).

In the same way, not all of us who are called after Christ, as they were after Israel, will be reckoned as belonging to the Christian race (*cf.* 1 Pet. 2:9), but only those who live according to His will, keep His commandments, and make up for their shortcomings with repentance. Judas Iscariot was not just one of those called, but one of the apostles, and not merely one of the apostles, but one of the company of the twelve chief apostles. But he was estranged from kinship with Christ and became of all men the most alienated from the name of Christ. Why? Because he did not hasten towards the kingdom of heaven that was being proclaimed, nor did he regard the extraordinary deeds and teaching of the Saviour. For when God's signs and works are understood, they lead those with the desire for knowledge of them to faith, and listening to holy instruction inspired by the truth that is in God reveals the way of life pleasing to God. With the help of both the miracles and the teaching, we can learn to despise bodily and earthly concerns, and lift up our minds to the hope laid up in heaven.

Judas, however, had no desire for these things, but looked towards the earth and theft, to earthly and detestable gains, and to the advantages he anticipated receiving from them for his flesh. He was a lover of what had been forbidden on many occasions and in many ways by the Father, Lord and Teacher of all. His kinship was not with Christ, nor with his fellow apostles at the time, but with those to whom the Lord had said, "Ye seek me, not because ye saw the miracles, but because ye did eat of the loaves, and were filled" (John 6:26). Having seen the miracles, eaten the bread, and heard the words of the enhypostatic Word made man for our sake, those people shouted to Pilate, "Away with him, away with him, crucify him" (John 19:15). In exactly the same way Judas, too, after seeing the Lord's majesty and divinity with his own eyes, and having more experience of it than others, handed Him over to those who sought to murder Him. But Christ was patient "unto death, even the death of the cross" (Phil. 2:8) – Oh inexpressible forbearance! – and in addition to triumphing over the prince of evil, He guides us towards patience and shows us that temptations and afflictions are for our good. "In affliction have we remembered thee", says the Scripture (*cf.* Isa. 26:16 LXX), and "I will bear the correction of the Lord" (*cf.* Mic. 7:9), and "Thy correction hath lifted me up" (*cf.* Ps. 18:35 LXX), that is to say, When I was bending down towards my body and its concerns, Your chastening raised me up and persuaded me to look towards You alone.

If, however, you do not run to God in times of trouble, and are not raised up by His correction, what other occasion, what else in existence or among creatures will serve to restore you? You may say that our bodies must have physical nourishment and other necessities. But of course; who can deny that? If you have these things in abundance, you obviously received them from God – "For what hast thou", asks the Scripture, "that thou didst not receive?" (1 Cor. 4:7) – so give thanks to the giver, express your gratitude through your actions. As He took your will into account and fulfilled your desire, so you too should draw near, heed His will, learn it thoroughly, obey it and put it into practice, that you may be praised for your wisdom: "Whosoever heareth", says the Lord, "these sayings of mine, and doeth them, I will liken him unto a wise man" (Matt. 7:24). From then on you will have Him as your generous benefactor, not only in respect of earthly, perishable goods, but also with regard to future heavenly gifts that endure. "Well done", He says, "thou good and faithful servant: thou hast been faithful over a few things, I will make thee ruler over many things: enter thou into the joy of thy lord" (Matt. 25:21). If, on the other hand, you do not have an abundance now of what your body needs, or fear that poverty lies ahead, again you should approach Him, again you should entreat Him, again you should obey Him. Because it says, "Obey the Lord and beseech him" (Ps. 37:7 LXX). Again therefore show yourself a good servant of His through your deeds. For He it is, according to the Psalms, "Who giveth them their meat in due season. Who openeth his hand, and satisfieth the desire of every living thing" (*cf.* Ps. 145:15–16). He says, "I shall not fail thee, nor forsake thee" (*cf.* Deut. 31:6), and "Behold, my servants shall eat", but He tells those who do not serve Him, "Ye shall be hungry" (Isa. 65:13).

Why do you imitate irrational animals in what is harmful to you, by stooping down towards your stomach and not looking up from earthly concerns, even though you were created upright, so that you might set your mind on heavenly things and seek what is above? Why do you want to be bound like that woman who was bent over because Satan had bound her for eighteen years (Luke 13:11–16), even though the Word of life (*cf.* 1 John 1:1) who released her can easily set you free and wishes to do so? Provided only that you run to Him, listen to Him and obey Him, and do not stop your ears, turn away or rebel.

Why do you copy brute beasts in this characteristic of theirs which is damaging to you, but not in what is to your advantage? Listen to the prophet saying that even lion cubs howl when they need food, and ask God for it and receive prey: "The young lions", he says, "roar after their prey, and seek their meat from God" (Ps. 104:21). By referring to lion cubs, he leaves those with understanding to deduce that this applies even more to other animals. For if lions, the most voracious, predatory and powerful of beasts, only have an abundance of prey when God gives it, what shall we say of other creatures? Christ, too, makes this same point in the gospel with regard to birds, saying, "Behold the fowls of the air: for they sow not, neither do they reap, nor gather into barns; yet your heavenly Father feedeth them" (Matt. 6:26). But why confine myself to animals on dry land, in the air, the sea, or even amphibians? If God, it says, so cares for and so decoratively and magnificently clothes "the grass of the field, which today is, and tomorrow is cast into the oven, and which neither toils nor spins; shall he not much more clothe and feed you, O ye of little faith?" (*cf.* Matt. 28–30).

Brethren, "Seek ye first the kingdom of God, and his righteousness", and not only will you be justified by His grace and become heirs of this perpetual kingdom of God for ever, but also, "all these things shall be added unto you" (Matt. 6:33). If, however, you do not seek God's kingdom and righteousness as a priority, but only those things which sustain this unstable body, you will not receive even what you seek, unless it be for the increase of your body's suffering and the eternal condemnation and loss of your soul.

This is demonstrated by the rich man who heard Abraham telling him, "Thou in thy lifetime receivedst thy good things" (Luke 16:25). Also, there was a time when the Jewish people wanted to eat meat in the wilderness, and God gave them quails in countless numbers (Num. 11:4, 31–33). "And they did eat, and were well filled: and he gave them their own desire. But while", it says, "their meat was yet in their mouths, the wrath of God came upon them, and slew them in their masses, and bound the chosen men of Israel hand and foot" (*cf.* Ps. 78:29–31 Lxx). Why did God's wrath strike them down "in their masses", that is kill large numbers of the multitude? On account of the fact that they complained against God and Moses, their leader appointed by God, and spoke against them. But why did He bind the chosen men of Israel? Because they did not restrain the multitude as they sank from bad to worse. Such men are driven out of the sacred Congregation and God's kingdom, whether they belong to the Old or New people of Israel. The Lord, too, points this out, saying in the gospels, "Many shall come from the east and the west and the north, and shall sit down with Abraham, and Isaac, and Jacob, in the kingdom of heaven. But the children of the kingdom shall be cast out into outer darkness" (*cf.* Matt. 8:11–12).

Who are those children of the kingdom expelled into darkness? Those who confess the faith, but deny God with their works, "being abominable, and disobedient, and unto every good work reprobate" (Titus 1:16). Who are those who sit down with Abraham, Isaac and Jacob in the heavenly kingdom? Those who, with sincere faith, order their lives according to the law and the teaching of the Spirit, and demonstrate their faith through their works.

If anyone wishes to be classed with the latter, delivered from outer darkness, deemed worthy of the unfading light of God's kingdom and to live for ever at rest with the saints in heaven, let him put off the old man, who is corrupt with deceitful lusts (*cf.* Eph. 4:22), these being drunkenness, fornication, adultery, impurity, covetousness, love of money, hatred, anger, slander and every evil passion. And through his deeds let him put on the new man renewed in the image of his Creator (*cf.* Col. 3:10), in which is charity, brotherly love, purity, self-control and every type of virtue. Through these Christ dwells within us, reconciling us with Himself and one another, to His glory and the glory of His Father without beginning, and of the co-eternal, life-giving Spirit, now and for ever and unto the ages of ages. Amen.

On the Old Testament Saints

DAVID INDICATES that our Lord Jesus Christ has no genealogy with regard to His divinity (Ps. 110:4), Isaiah says the same (Isa. 53:8), and later so does the apostle (Heb. 7:3). How can the descent be traced of Him "who is in the beginning, and is with God, and is God, and is the Word and Son of God" (*cf.* John 1:1–2, 18)? He does not have a Father who was before Him, and shares with His Father "a name which is above every name" and all speech (Phil. 2:9). For the most part, genealogies are traced back through different surnames; but there is no surname for God (*cf.* Gen. 32:29), and whatever may be said of Father, Son and Holy Spirit, They are one and do not differ in any respect.

Impossible to recount is Christ's descent according to His divinity, but His ancestry according to His human nature can be traced, since He who deigned to become Son of man in order to save mankind was the offspring of men. And it is this genealogy of His that two of the evangelists, Matthew and Luke, recorded. But although Matthew, in the passage from his Gospel read today, begins with those born first, he makes no mention of anyone before Abraham. He traces the line down from Abraham until he reaches Joseph to whom, by divine dispensation, the Virgin Mother of God was betrothed (Matt. 1:1–16), being of the same tribe and homeland as him, that her own stock might be shown from this to be in no way inferior. Luke, by contrast, begins not with the earliest forebears but the most recent, and working his way back from Joseph the Betrothed, does not stop at Abraham, nor, having included Abraham's predecessors, does he end with Adam, but lists God among Christ's human forebears (Luke 3:23–38); wishing to show, in my opinion, that from the beginning man was not just a creation of God, but also a son in the Spirit, which was given to him at the same time as his soul, through God's quickening breath (Gen. 2:7). It was granted to him as a pledge that, if, waiting patiently for it, he kept the commandment, he would be able to share through the same Spirit in a more perfect union with God, by which he would live for ever with Him and obtain immortality.

By heeding the evil counsel of the pernicious angel, man transgressed the divine commandments, was shown to be unworthy, forfeited the pledge and interrupted God's plan. God's grace, however, is unalterable and His purpose cannot prove false, so some of man's offspring were chosen, that, from among many, a suitable receptacle for this divine adoption and grace might be found, who would serve God's will perfectly, and would be revealed as a vessel worthy to unite divine and human nature in one person, not just exalting our nature, but restoring the human race. The holy Maid and Virgin Mother of God was this vessel, so she was proclaimed by the archangel Gabriel as full of grace (Luke 1:28), being the chosen one among the chosen, blameless, undefiled and worthy to contain the person of the God-man and to collaborate with Him. Therefore God pre-ordained her before all ages, chose her from among all who had ever lived, and deemed her worthy of more grace than anyone else, making her the holiest of saints, even before her mysterious childbearing. For that reason, He graciously willed that she should make her home in the Holy of Holies, and accepted her as His companion to share His dwelling from her childhood. He did not simply choose her from the masses, but from the elect of all time, who were admired and renowned for their piety and wisdom, and for their character, words and deeds, which pleased God and brought benefit to all.

Note where this choice began. The excellent Seth was chosen from among Adam's children, because by his well-ordered conduct, his control over his senses and his glorious virtue he showed himself to be a living heaven and so came to be one of the elect, from whom the Virgin would spring forth, that truly heavenly and divinely appropriate chariot of the supracelestial God, and through whom He would call men back to eternal sonship. Therefore all Seth's stock were called sons of God (*cf.* Gen. 6:2), because it was from this race that the Son of God was to become the Son of man. That is why the name Seth can be interpreted to mean "resurrection", or rather "a rising up from", which really refers to the Lord, who promises and gives eternal life to those who believe in Him.

And how worthy a type of Christ is Seth? "Seth was born to Eve", as she herself says, "instead of Abel" (*cf.* Gen. 4:25), whom Cain envied and murdered, whereas the Virgin's son, Christ, was born to the human race instead of Adam, whom the prince and father of evil killed out of envy. Seth, however, did not raise up Abel, as he was merely a prefiguration of the resurrection, whereas our Lord Jesus Christ resurrected Adam, for He is the true life and resurrection of mankind (*cf.* John 11:25), through whom Seth's descendants were deemed worthy, in hope, of divine adoption, being called sons of God. That they were referred to as God's sons on account of this hope, is demonstrated by the first person to be so called and to inherit God's election. This was Seth's son Enos who, as Moses wrote, "was the first to hope to be called by the Lord's name" (*cf.* Gen. 4:26 Lxx).

Do you see clearly that it was through hope that he came to be so called? If the Seventy say, "He was the first to hope to call upon the Lord's name", they are not at all in disagreement with the others; because Enos lived in a way that pleased God more than anyone else in his day, and was the first to receive this hope from God. He called upon this hope and was called after it. Seth was chosen by God from among Adam's sons, and so Luke, in preparing his genealogy, traces back to him the whole race from which Christ was born according to the flesh. Then Enos was chosen in preference to Seth's other children, as we have said. From his descendants Enoch was chosen, who proved through what happened to him that virtue does not go unrewarded, and that this fleeting world is not worthy of those who are well-pleasing to God, for he was translated because he pleased God (Gen. 5:24, Heb. 11:5). Lamech was chosen and preferred to Enoch's other descendants, and after him his son, Noah, attained to God's election and became the only father of everyone in the world after the flood. Only he and his entire family were found to live chastely at that time when the sons of God took wives from among the daughters of men, as Moses tells us (Gen. 6:1–2). This means that among the offspring of Seth, the forefather of the Mother of God, those who were rejected as unworthy were swept out of the Virgin Mother's family and completely deprived of the divine Spirit. Later this Spirit came upon the Virgin, according to the angel's words to her: "The Holy Ghost shall come upon thee, and the power of the Highest shall overshadow thee" (Luke 1:35). The Spirit also arranged beforehand for the Virgin to come into being, choosing from the beginning, and cleansing, the line of her descent, accepting those who were worthy, or were to become fathers of eminent men, but utterly casting out the unworthy.

This is why the Lord God said on that occasion of those rejected ones, "My spirit shall not abide with these men, for they are flesh" (*cf.* Gen. 6:3 LXX). Although the Virgin, of whom Christ was born according to the flesh, came from Adam's flesh and seed, yet, because this flesh had been cleansed in many different ways by the Holy Spirit from the start, she was descended from those who had been chosen from every generation for their excellence. Noah, too, "a just man and perfect in his generation", as the Scriptures say of him (Gen. 6:9), was found worthy of this election.

Observe also that the Holy Spirit makes it clear to such as have understanding that the whole of divinely inspired Scripture was written because of the Virgin Mother of God. It relates in detail the entire line of her ancestry, which begins with Adam, then passes through Seth, Noah and Abraham, as well as David and Zerubbabel, those in between them and their successors, and goes up to the time of the Virgin Mother of God. By contrast, Scripture does not touch upon some races at all, and in the case of others, it makes a start at tracing their descent, then soon abandons them, leaving them in the depths of oblivion. Above all, it commemorates those of the Mother of God's forebears who, in their own lives and the deeds wrought by them, prefigured Christ, who was to be born of the Virgin.

See how Noah clearly foreshadows Him who was later to be born of the Virgin, for whose sake the election was made. For Noah was shown to be the saviour, not of all the race of men in general, but of his own household, all of whom were saved through him. In the same way Christ, too, is the Saviour of the race of men, not of all men in general, but of all His own household, that is of His Church; not, however, of the disobedient. Furthermore, the name Noah can be translated to mean "rest" (*cf.* Gen. 5:29). But who is true "rest" except the Virgin's Son, who says, "Come unto me through repentance, all ye that labour and are heavy laden with sins, and I will give you rest" (*cf.* Matt. 11:28), bestowing freedom, ease and eternal life upon you.

Lamech, who gave Noah this name, because he saw in him Christ, who was later to come from their stock, and would be the comfort of all God-fearing people down through the ages, clearly prophesied through this name concerning Christ. "He called his name Noah", says the Scripture, "saying, This same shall bring us rest from our works, and from the toils of our hands, and from the earth, which the Lord our God hath cursed" (Gen. 5:29 Lxx). These words are not about the flood which came to pass, for Lamech's death preceded the flood, yet he says that Noah will "bring us rest", including himself as a partaker in the comfort he foretold. In those days it had not yet come about that in each man "every imagination of the thoughts of his heart was only evil continually" (Gen. 6:5) throughout his life, which was why the universal destruction of everyone on earth came upon the earth from God. So to whom do his words refer when he says, "He will bring us rest?" He also says, "He shall bring us rest from the earth, which God hath cursed". Who else gives us rest from this earth except Him who opened heaven, raised our nature thither and taught us, through words and deeds, the way up to heaven, calling us towards it? But if the flood too prefigured this rest, it did so by cutting off sins and laying them to rest, not by bringing comfort and ease to sinners.

In this way and for these reasons, Noah attained to God's election. Of his children, Shem was accepted among those chosen to be the blessed family of the Mother of God. That is why, although Japheth also appears to have been well-pleasing to his father, only Shem heard from his father, "Blessed be the Lord God of Shem" (Gen. 9:26), as his progeny was to be divine. For it was from him that Abraham was descended, who was preferred according to God's election above all Shem's offspring and was called to be part of the lineage of the Virgin Mother. He was given a new name by God, and received that great promise that all the families of the earth would be blessed in his seed (Gen. 17:5; 12:3). According to Paul, Christ our God, who was born of the Virgin is his seed according to the flesh (Gal. 3:16). And who could describe the divine visions that Abraham experienced, or the signs and promises from God which foreshadowed and prophesied concerning the ever-virgin Mother of God and her ineffable childbearing? Let us, however, quickly pass over what happened next, as time does not permit us to speak at length. From among Abraham's children Isaac was chosen, then Jacob from among his sons, and the tribe of Judah from Jacob's offspring. From this tribe the root of Jesse was selected, and from those who sprang from this root, David the psalmist and prophet and king, of whom God says, "Thy seed shall endure for ever, and his throne as the sun before me; and as the moon that is established for ever, and the witness in heaven is faithful" (*cf.* Ps. 89:36–37 LXX).

Who is this witness? Obviously He who sits upon the heavenly throne, of whom it says elsewhere: "His name shall be continued as long as the sun: and all the families of the earth shall be blessed in him" (Ps. 72:17 LXX). From this the lineage of the Mother of God and Joseph, to whom she was betrothed, seems somehow double, for both were of the same tribe and descent according to the law. Thus the family's ancestral line is twofold, made up both of natural children and children according to the law, often converging into one, but sometimes divided into two, so that the same child, strange as it may seem, might be the son of two fathers who are brothers, of the one from a legal point of view, as not having been begotten of him physically, and of the other, according to nature, as having been raised up as seed for his brother (*cf.* Matt. 22:24, Deut. 25:5–6, Gen. 38:8); inasmuch as the child traces his ancestry back to David through both his fathers. It is possible to see the dual nature of this lineage in another respect, because the royal line was united on many occasions and in numerous ways with the priestly one. Thus in the holy ancestral line of the Mother of God, Zerubbabel traces his lineage back to David through the descendants of Nathan, who was counted among the priests, as well as through those of Solomon, who inherited the kingdom. For this reason the Lord's genealogy according to the flesh is drawn up differently by the evangelists Luke and Matthew, because one takes into account natural fathers, the other, fathers according to the law, and one mentions only those of royal descent, whereas Luke brings in those of the Levitical race and those of the royal house, who were bound together by priesthood or marriage.

As for Zerubbabel, because he was also favoured among the Mother of God's forebears, he too prefigured Christ and was honoured with great titles and authority. Born in captivity, he was admired by Cyrus, king of the Medes and Persians, for his virtue and understanding. He taught both Hebrews and foreigners the power of the truth, set his race free from servitude and restored God's Temple (1 Esd. 4:33–63, Ezra 3:1–13). Later Christ did something similar, not renewing the inanimate Temple, but that living, rational temple, our nature, and redeeming it, not from perceptible and temporary, but spiritual and primeval captivity. Nor did he move His followers from one country to another, but transferred them from earth to heaven. Zerubbabel was the forefather of both the Virgin and Joseph to whom she was betrothed, but whereas he was the Virgin's forebear by nature alone, he was Joseph's according to nature and the law. For Joseph had two fathers, Heli according to Luke (Luke 3:23), and Jacob according to Matthew (Matt. 1:16). Heli and Jacob were brothers descended from Zerubbabel, and when Heli died without children, Jacob fathered a child, Joseph, by his brother's wife, who according to the law belonged to Heli.

Now these things are examples and types of greater mysteries, since it was necessary that the royal line be united in many ways with the priestly race, which would bring forth the family of Christ according to the flesh; because in many ways Christ is truly the eternal King and High Priest. And the fact that adopted sons are counted as sons, that the law approves of adoptive fathers no less and sometimes more than natural fathers, and that the same, appropriately, applies to other kinds of kinship, was a clear example and type of our adoption by Christ, our kinship with Him and our calling according to the Spirit and the law of grace. For the Lord Himself says in the Gospels, "Whosoever shall do the will of my Father which is in heaven, the same is my brother, and sister, and mother" (Matt. 12:50).

Do you see that the family and kin of Christ are not engendered according to nature, but according to grace and the law that comes from grace? This law is so far superior to the law given through Moses that, whereas those called sons according to the law of Moses are neither born of God nor do they transcend human nature, those styled sons by the law of grace are born of God, brought to perfection above nature and made sons of Abraham through Christ, more closely associated with him than sons according to blood. All who have been baptized into Christ have put on Christ, according to Paul (Gal. 3:27), and although they are other people's children according to nature, they are born supernaturally of Christ, who in this way conquers nature. For as He became incarnate without seed of the Holy Spirit and the ever-virgin Mary, so He grants potential and power to those who believe in His name to become children of God. For "as many as received him", says the evangelist, "to them gave he power to become the sons of God, even to them that believe on his name: which were born, not of blood, nor of the will of the flesh, nor of the will of man, but of God" (John 1:12–13).

Why, when he says, "which were born of God", does he not say "and became sons of God", but "received power to become" sons? Because he was looking towards the end and the universal restoration, the perfection of the age to come. The same evangelist says in his Epistles, "It doth not yet appear what we shall be: but when he shall appear, we shall be like him" (1 John 3:2). Then shall we be children of God, seeing and experiencing God's radiance, with the rays of Christ's glory shining around us and shining ourselves, as Moses and Elijah proved to us when they appeared with Him in glory on Mount Tabor (Matt. 17:3, Luke 9:30). "The righteous", it says, "shall shine forth as the sun in the kingdom of their Father" (Matt. 13:43). We receive power for this purpose now through the grace of divine baptism. Just as a newborn infant has received potential from his parents to become a man and heir to their house and fortune, but does not yet possess that inheritance because he is a minor, nor will he receive it if he dies before coming of age, so a person born again in the Spirit through Christian baptism has received power to become a son and heir of God, a joint-heir with Christ (*cf.* Rom. 8:17), and in the age to come he will, with all certainty, receive the divine and immortal adoption as a son, which will not be taken from him, unless he has forfeited this by spiritual death. Sin is spiritual death, and whereas physical death is annulled when the future age arrives, spiritual death is confirmed for those who bring it with them from here.

Everyone who has been baptized, if he is to obtain the eternal blessedness and salvation for which he hopes, should live free from all sin. Peter and Paul, the leaders of the highest company of the holy apostles made this clear. Paul said of Christ, "In that he died, he died unto sin once: but in that he liveth, he liveth unto God", adding, "likewise we also ought to be dead indeed unto sin, but alive unto God" (*cf.* Rom. 6:10–11), whereas Peter wrote, "Forasmuch then as Christ hath died for us in the flesh, arm yourselves likewise with the same mind: that ye no longer should live the rest of your time by the lusts of men, but by the will of God" (*cf.* 1 Pet. 4:1–2). If it was for our sake that the Lord lived His time on earth, to leave us an example, and He passed His life without sin, we too must live without sin, in imitation of Him. Since He said even to Abraham's descendants according to the flesh, "If ye were Abraham's children, ye would do the works of Abraham" (John 8:39), how much more will He say to us who have no physical kinship with Him, "If you were My children, you would do My works"? It is therefore consistent and just that anyone who, after divine baptism, after the covenants he made then to God and the grace he received from it, does not follow Christ's way of life step by step, but transgresses and offends against the benefactor, should be utterly deprived of divine adoption and the eternal inheritance.

But, O Christ our King, who can worthily extol the greatness of Your love for mankind? What was unnecessary for Him and what He did not do, namely, repentance (for He never needed to repent, being sinless, *cf.* Heb. 4:15), He granted to us as a mediator for when we sin even after receiving grace. Repentance means returning once again to Him and to a life according to His will out of remorse. Even if someone commits a deadly sin, if he turns away from it with all his soul, abstains from it and turns back to the Lord in deed and truth, he should take courage and be of good hope, for he shall not lose eternal life and salvation. When a child according to the flesh meets his death, he is not brought back to life by his father, but someone born of Christ, even though he fall into deadly sins, if he turns again and runs to the Father who raises the dead, is made alive once more, obtains divine adoption, and is not cast out from the company of the just.

May we all attain to this, to the glory of Christ and of His Father without beginning and of the life-giving Spirit, now and for ever, and unto unceasing ages. Amen.

On Saint John the Baptist

If the death of the saints is precious (Ps. 116:15) and the just are remembered with praise (Prov. 10:7 Lxx), it is even more fitting for us to commemorate John, the highest summit of holy and righteous men, by extolling him. He leapt in the womb in anticipation of the Word of God who took flesh for our sake (Luke 1:41); he was His Forerunner and went before Him as His herald, and the Lord in turn proclaimed and bore witness that John was superior to all the prophets, saints and just men down through the ages (*cf.* Luke 7:28). Everything about him surpasses human speech, and the only-begotten Son of God witnessed to him and honoured him, and he has no need of any tribute from us. But this does not mean that we should keep silent and fail to honour with our words, as best we can, the one whom the Scriptures refer to as "the voice" of the sublime Word (Matt. 3:3, *cf.* Isa. 40:3 Lxx). On the contrary, the fact that he was proclaimed to be so great and witnessed to by Christ, the Lord of all, should move every tongue to sing his praises as much as it can. Not that we can add to his glory in any way – how could we? – but in order to pay our debt individually and together by recounting the wonders surrounding him and celebrating them in song.

The whole life of the greatest man born of woman was a supreme miracle. John was a prophet and much more than a prophet (Luke 7:26), even before he was born; and not only did his entire life transcend all wonders, but so did everything concerning him, both long before his lifetime and afterwards. The divine predictions of seers inspired by God described him as an angel rather than a man (Matt. 11:10, *cf.* Exod. 23:20, Mal. 3:1), as a lampstand for the light (John 5:35, *cf.* Ps. 132:17), a divinely radiant star bringing in the morning (*cf.* John 1:8; 5:35), for he went before the Sun of righteousness (Mal. 4:2), and was "the voice" of God's Word (Matt. 3:3, *cf.* Isa. 40:3 LXX). What could be closer or more akin to God the Word than God's voice?

When the time for his conception drew near it was not a man but an angel who flew down from heaven and put an end to Zacharias and Elizabeth's barrenness, promising that the couple who had been childless from their youth would bear a child in extreme old age. The birth of this son would, he foretold, cause much joy, as it would be for the salvation of all (Luke 1:13–14). "For he", said the angel, "shall be great in the sight of the Lord, and shall be filled with the Holy Ghost, even from his mother's womb. And many of the children of Israel shall he turn to the Lord their God. And he shall go before him in the spirit and power of Elias" (Luke 1:15–17). For he shall be a virgin as Elijah was, and dwell in the desert more than he did; and he shall censure kings and queens who transgress. What puts him above Elijah, however, is that he shall be the Forerunner of God, for the Scripture says, "He shall go before him".

Because Zacharias considered these things beyond belief, his tongue was tied. Since he did not want to announce voluntarily the child's mysterious conception, he proclaimed it against his will by being silent until he saw "the voice" of the Word coming into the light (Luke 1:18–22, 76–79). Having been conceived with so many great promises, he was anointed as a prophet before being born and – marvellous to relate! – passed on this anointing to his mother (Luke 1:41–45). Like Isaiah, he was clothed in the "garment of salvation" and the "robe of righteousness" (Isa. 61:10); like Elijah he anointed someone else to be a prophet in his place (*cf.* 1 Kgs. 19:16), and while still unborn he equalled and surpassed both prophets in their perfection, because he displayed these attributes in the presence of the Lord. Once an unborn babe's members have been formed, it can move, but does not yet have a voice, as it is not yet living in the air. When the Virgin, who was at that time carrying God within her, appeared, even though John was in the womb he did not fail to perceive God's presence and His dispensation, but extolled it, declaring the divinity through his mother's tongue (Luke 1:42). He leapt and rejoiced within her as – what a miracle! – he received in the Holy Spirit the fullness of the age to come in his mother's womb.

Proclaiming beforehand the mystery of eternal life, the great Paul says, "It is sown a natural body; it is raised a spiritual body" (1 Cor. 15:44). That is to say, the body will be indwelt and motivated by the supernatural power of the divine Spirit in the age to come. In the same way, John was sown and shaped in his mother's womb as a natural body, but by the mysterious anointing of the Holy Spirit while he was within her, he was shown to be a spiritual body, who leapt and rejoiced in the Spirit and made his mother a prophetess. Through her tongue he blessed God with a loud voice and declared the Virgin who was with child to be the Mother of the Lord, and He addressed her unborn Babe as the fruit of her womb, proving that she was at the same time both pregnant and a virgin (Luke 1:41–45).

John did not merely, in the words of the Scripture, choose the good before knowing evil (*cf.* Isa. 7:16 LXX), but while still unborn, before knowing the world, he surpassed it. Then once he was born he delighted and amazed everyone by reason of the miraculous events surrounding him, because, it says, "The hand of the Lord was with him" (Luke 1:66), working wonders again as it had in earlier time. His father's mouth, which had been closed because he had not believed in the child's strange conception, was opened and filled with the Holy Spirit, and he prophesied, among other things, about this his son, saying, "And thou, child shalt be called the prophet of the Highest: for thou shalt go before the face of the Lord to prepare his ways; to give knowledge of salvation unto his people" (Luke 1:76–77). Once this divine child, this living instrument of grace from his mother's womb, had been conceived, he was moved by grace to rejoice in the Holy Spirit. In the same way, after being born, he grew and waxed strong in the Spirit (Luke 1:80). As the world was unworthy of him, he dwelt continuously in desert places from his earliest years, leading a frugal life without cares or worldly concerns, a stranger to sadness, free from coarse passions and above base, material pleasure, which merely beguiles the body and its senses. He lived for God alone, beholding only God and making God his delight. It was as if he lived somewhere exalted above the earth. "And he was in the deserts", it says, "till the day of his shewing unto Israel" (Luke 1:80).

On what day was he shown to Israel? When the time came for the Lord to be baptized, concerning which time the Scripture says, "there is none that understandeth, there is none that seeketh after God. They are all gone out of the way, they are together become unprofitable" (Rom. 3:11, *cf.* Ps. 14:3 and 53: *cf.* 53:2–3 LXX). Just as in those days the Lord came down from heaven for our sake, when we were all ungodly (*cf.* Rom. 5:6–8), because of His ineffable love, so John left the desert for our sake to minister to the Lord's loving purpose. As men's wickedness was then at its peak, and the loving condescension of God was beyond compare, a servant was also needed, whose virtue was nothing less than excellent, so that he could draw observers, as John did, having attracted their admiration as someone unusual with a superhuman way of life. And the message he preached was worthy of the manner in which he lived, for he proclaimed the kingdom of heaven, threatened unquenchable fire, and taught that Christ was the heavenly King, "Whose fan is in his hand, and he will throughly purge his floor, and will gather the wheat into his garner; but the chaff he will burn with fire unquenchable" (Luke 3:17).

He did not just make the Lord known to all with his words, but also through his deeds. He baptized Him, pointed Him out with his finger, recommended Him to his own disciples, and bore witness in all ways that this man was the Son of the Father, the Lamb of God (*cf.* John 1:29, 34–36), the bridegroom of the souls that draw near to Him (John 3:29), He who bears the sin of the world (John 1:29), takes away defilement, and brings instead His gift of sanctification.

Once John had prepared the Lord's way, according to Zacharias's prophecy, had fulfilled everything which he had been sent to do, had gone before Him, and had baptized Him in the Jordan, he conceded to Christ the rôle of addressing the assembled crowds and teaching them, and withdrew from the multitude, handing them over to the Lord. As Herod, the son of that Herod who slaughtered the infants (Matt. 2:16), had not succeeded to all his father's power, being merely a tetrarch, but had exceeded him in evil, living in immorality and presenting the Jews with an example of wickedness, John was unable to keep silent. (How could he, as he was "the voice" of the Truth? Matt. 3:3, *cf.* Isa. 40:3 LXX.) He accused him on account of his other evil deeds, but especially concerning Herodias, his brother's wife, whom he had seized and illegally wed. "It is not lawful", said John to Herod, "for thee to have thy brother Philip's wife" (Mark 6:18). Finding reproach, or rather, the reproaches, unbearable, he added this to his other evil acts, that he shut up John in prison (Luke 3:20).

Philip was also Herod's son, and was tetrarch of another region. After the cruel murder of the infants had deranged their father, Herod (Matt. 2:16), he fell victim to misfortunes and incurable, unbearable illnesses, and out of extreme folly and great pain he killed himself. It was then that the angel said to Joseph in Egypt, "Arise, and take the young child and his mother, and go into the land of Israel: for they are dead which sought the young child's life" (Matt. 2:20). When this Herod's life came to an evil end, Caesar, who held universal authority at that time, divided Herod's realm into four portions. He put other men in charge of two of them, but made Herod's sons, Philip and Herod, tetrarchs of the remaining parts. That is why the evangelist Luke says that Herod was tetrarch of Galilee, and his brother Philip tetrarch of Ituraea and the region of Trachonitis when John appeared by the Jordan preaching the baptism of repentance (Luke 3:1–3).

It was this young Herod who, as Matthew and Mark relate, laid hold of John, and bound him, and put him in prison, because he had been accused by John on account of Herodias, his brother's wife, whom he had taken as his own (Matt. 14:3, Mark 6:17). Luke says that Herod, being reproved not just on account of Herodias, but "for all the evils which he had done, added yet this above all, that he shut up John in prison" (Luke 3:19–20). Why do the other evangelists refer only to the accusation concerning Herodias? John was shut up in prison for many other reasons as well, especially because of all those actions of the evilly-inclined King, for which he had been rebuked by John, and so could not bear him to speak freely. However, the sole cause of John's head being cut off was the adulteress, who by her own efforts and wiles accomplished the deed and saw it through to its conclusion. She inwardly cherished malice against John, who was reproving and opposing Herod for his unlawful act, and she wanted to kill him (Mark 6:19), for there was no other way to silence what she took to be an accusation against herself. The abomination in which she was involved did not have just one or two aspects, but was highly complex. It was a matter of adultery, the most shameful of sins, and adultery committed by none other than the brother of the adulteress's husband, the father of her daughter, while the daughter was still alive. Even if the husband had died, his brother could not marry the widow according to the law of Moses (*cf.* Deut. 25:5, Gen. 38:8), but Herod secretly planned their union while his brother was alive and had a daughter. Nor did he do this shameful deed secretly or with any sort of dissimulation, but accomplished the abomination openly and shamelessly.

Completely given over to evil in this way, and unable to endure censure, he shut up John in prison. But this imprisonment itself became an even greater reproach to him, as people heard about it and saw it, and the news circulated everywhere. As a result, Herodias deeply resented John, and inwardly wanted to murder him, but could not. "For Herod", it says, "feared John, knowing that he was a just man and an holy" (Mark 6:20). Although Herod feared John on account of his outstanding virtue, he had no fear of God, from whom men receive virtue. Also, even though he knew him to be a just and holy man, he did not fear John in his own right, but feared him because of the masses, who, as Matthew tells us, "counted him as a prophet" (Matt. 14:5). According to his account, not just Herodias, but also Herod himself wanted to put him to death, but feared the multitude.

The meaning of Mark's statement, that Herod heard John gladly is as follows: In the case of medicinal draughts, we are aware of their bitter taste, but we take them, because we understand they do us good. But the opposite applies to spiritual teachings. As they are naturally sweet, even those who do not believe in them delight in them, but they do not accept them, because they realize that they are opposed to their own evil desires. Perhaps earlier on Herod had heard John gladly, since, as it says, "he observed him; and when he heard him, he did many things" (Mark 6:20). But as evil men naturally hate their accusers, since reproof gives rise to hatred, he ignored all this, agreed with the adulteress's murderous purpose, and would himself have put John to death, according to Matthew, but feared the multitude (Matt. 14:5). It was not that he dreaded some sort of resistance on their part, but just that they would condemn him, because they counted John as a prophet. He knew that everyone was aware of John's virtue and grace, and, being reliant on the good opinion of the common people, he feared their criticism. As he was seeking praise from them, in some respects he still feigned obedience and reverence towards John.

Herodias, however, who was wise in doing evil, put an end to this fear of Herod's, and persuaded him to murder John without just cause, in accordance with her own opinion, or rather, her deceit. Full of spite and murderous feelings, she was looking for an opportunity to put into effect her fanatical hatred of the Baptist and Prophet, while protecting herself from being blamed by the masses. "And when", it says, "a convenient day was come" (Mark 6:21), convenient, that is, for the murderous scheme, during the celebration of Herod's birthday, while all the people were assembled, and the men of importance were in their seats, Herodias's daughter came in among them all, despatched by her mother for this purpose (Mark 6:22). The girl danced in the sight of all, and pleased everyone including Herod. Given that she was Herodias' daughter, and had been sent in by her, how could she fail either to dance shamelessly, or to please Herod? Her brazen dancing so captivated the pleasure-loving King that he said to the girl, "Ask of me whatsoever thou wilt, and I will give it thee. And he sware unto her, Whatsoever thou shalt ask of me, I will give it thee, unto the half of my kingdom" (Mark 6:22–23).

The impudent girl went out to her mother, the one who had taught her how to leap and writhe in that unseemly way, and told her of the oath. She asked to be instructed as to what she should request, was immediately informed, and eagerly obeyed (Mark 6:24). She hurried back to the King, and shamelessly stated her demand, saying, "I will that thou give me at once", that is, as quickly as possible, this very moment, "in a charger the head of John the Baptist" (Mark 6:25). This is what the girl asked for without blushing, and the adulteress imagined that by such means she would prevent the king being blamed for murdering the Baptist and Prophet, for she said that he would appear to be committing the murder out of respect for this oath, not out of hatred for the righteous man. "And the king", it says, "was exceedingly sorry: yet for his oath's sake, and for their sakes which sat with him, he would not reject her". So he sent and beheaded John in prison, and the head was brought and given to the girl (Mark 6:2:26–28).

How many evils are caused by the mad desire for glory! Herod was unable to murder John because of the multitude, but he did it on account of the people sitting with him. He was exceeding sorry for the sole reason that he thought he had lost the esteem of the masses. The King was indeed hemmed in on every side. If he murdered the just man, he could expect to be blamed for the murder. If he did not, he would seem to have broken his oath. The oath was the result of pride, his fear of breaking it was due to conceit, and the murder committed to keep it was for honour's sake. It was vainglory which assembled that whole drinking party. The Lord is right to say in the Gospels, "How can ye believe in me, which receive honour one of another, and seek not the honour that cometh from God only" (John 5:44). Because the Jews too looked for glory from men, they refused to believe in Him. They beheaded all their prophets, and destroyed Christ, the fulfilment of the prophets. The actions of a king ruled over by adulteresses and dancing girls were just as bad.

He was enchanted and pleased by such evil deeds, and because of them he sold and betrayed his kingdom, and was brought to the point of doing an act such as this.

Brethren, our mind too suffers something similar. It was created by God to be king and absolute ruler of the passions, but when charmed by them, it is led into unnatural servitude and alien deeds. All those enslaved by sin and passions, when they are accused by their own conscience, are grieved and displeased. Their first reaction is, so to speak, to shut their conscience, as Herod imprisoned John, because he did not want to hear him. They cannot even bear to hear words of Scripture which reject sin, and encourage every kind of goodness. Finally, once they are completely in the power of the Herodias, who unlawfully shares their life – in other words, of a mind that is prone to sin – they destroy the word of grace dwelling within them, that is, their conscience. Annulling it utterly, they disbelieve and contradict the Scripture inspired by God, becoming entirely unscrupulous and opposed to God's word, as Herod was against John.

Those who speak against the truth of godliness also suffer the same fate, and, to an even greater extent, do the same things. Standing accused by the prophetic, apostolic and patristic words which we offer, initially it is as if they shut them up in books, saying, "Let them stay in there, and may nobody use them or pronounce them", for they do not listen to the Lord who tells us, "Search the scriptures; for in them ye shall find eternal life" (*cf.* John 5:39). Subsequently, led into something worse by Herodias, their own impious imagination, they serve them up slaughtered on a plate, destroyed by their own writings, for the malicious joy of those who agree with them, and to their detriment.

Herod, therefore, is an example of everything evil and impious, whereas John is the pillar of all virtue and godliness. Herod is the fullness of wickedness, the power of ungodliness, the tool of lawlessness, is absolutely carnal, and lives and thinks according to the flesh. John, by contrast, is the summit of all the God-bearing men down through the ages, the visible resting-place of the gifts of the Spirit, who bears the Name of divine grace, and in whom all piety and virtue dwell. Two images are set before us today, extreme opposites at odds with each other. The one seems to bring a little enjoyment and honour in the short term to those inclined to live after its example, then delivers them up to unceasing, unbearable disgrace and affliction. The other gives those who look towards it short-lived suffering, then bestows on them glory and divine enjoyment, which are beyond description, true and eternal. If we live after the flesh, imitating the carnal Herod, we shall die, as the apostle says (Rom. 8:13). But if, through the divine Spirit and with zeal like John's, we oppose the body's evil appetites and deeds, we shall live for ever.

The outcome of living according to the Spirit "is hidden now in Christ with God", and is not yet obvious to all. But when He appears (*cf.* Col. 3:3–4), "we shall be like Him" (1 John 3:2), "heirs of God, joint-heirs with Christ" (Rom. 8:17), and shall attain to those everlasting and incorruptible good things, "which eye has not seen, nor ear heard, neither have they entered into the heart of man" (*cf.* 1 Cor. 2:9), for they transcend hearing, sight, and understanding. As for those who live according to the flesh, their pleasures are not just fleeting and temporary, but so slight and paltry that they can be compared to the husks eaten by pigs (*cf.* Luke 15:16).

Even if these carnal pleasures were everlasting, we would still of necessity prefer spiritual joys to them, since these are in all respects incomparably more excellent. If, on the other hand, fleshly delights were as great and amazing as spiritual ones, the fact that the former are transitory and the latter eternal would again make the latter preferable because they endure. As spiritual pleasures are both everlasting and beyond compare, and the delights of the flesh are pointless and short-lived, let us, brethren, prefer those which are permanent, ineffable and heavenly, rather than those which are swept away and go to ruin. Let us overlook things that are fleeting, even if they treacherously beguile our senses for a moment, and let us lay claim to the lasting and eternally indestructible good things to come. We should flee from being like Herod and strive as much as we can to imitate the Forerunner's grace, especially those of us who live as monks, whose manner of life is set apart, and is more akin to the solitary life of the Prophet and Baptist in the desert. As a prophet, he foresaw that it would be the order of monks who would be able to some extent to emulate him, and his head was cut off as he struggled, not for the sake of godliness, but for virtue, so that we too might be ready to resist sin to the point of death, in the knowledge that he who puts the passions to flight through virtue will receive a martyr's crown. Just as sin is a lesser evil compared with godlessness, so it follows that putting yourself at risk for virtue's sake is even better than doing so for godliness. For anyone who lays down his life in this lesser cause of virtue could not fail to do the same, had the need arisen, in the greater cause of godliness.

That is why the greatest "among them that are born of women" (Matt. 11:11), the preacher of repentance and the Lord's Prophet and Herald, had his head cut off in the struggle for virtue. Nor was he just the Forerunner of Christ, but also of His Church and particularly, brethren, of our monastic way of life. He was born of Elizabeth, a barren woman, and we were born of the Church of the Gentiles of whom it is written, "Sing, O barren, thou that didst not bear; break forth into singing, and cry aloud, thou that didst not travail with child: for more are the children of the desolate than the children of the married wife" (Isa. 54:1, Gal. 4:27). After John was born, Herod, the murderer of infants, pursued him with murderous intent, fighting against him out of hatred for Christ, but the Forerunner found refuge in the desert, which he loved more than the world, and there he dwelt. In the same way, the Herod of our minds attacks us after our spiritual birth, persecuting Christ now through us.

So let us too flee from the world, and take refuge in those schools of virtue dedicated to God, that we may escape from Herod's pitiless soldiers armed with spears and swords, who stir up the passions, by means of which he inflicts spiritual death, separating men from God. This is the death that comes upon us through the windows of our senses. It came about originally by means of these senses, and dragged down the human race, banishing our forebears from eternal life. Eve heard the evil one's malicious counsel: she saw, succumbed, ate, died, enticed the man, and shared the taste and the fall with him. Incapable of withstanding a single trial, they immediately gave heed to a treacherous word, and were overcome by a beautiful sight, although they were not yet subject to the passions but dispassionate, wandering about in a place free from passions. So do you think that we, who have been born and brought up in the world, can avoid being harmed, or suffering wounds and a change for the worse in our inner selves, when we are faced with the passions in their various guises, and with hearing and joining in prolonged and unseemly conversations? That would be absolutely impossible.

For these reasons the Fathers imitated the Forerunner of grace, bade farewell to the world, and fled the company of those devoted to it. Some inhabited the desert and attracted to it many of those born later. Others led ascetic lives within sacred enclosures and organized spiritual communities, and we associate ourselves with various ones of these in emulation of the Fathers, and live in these hallowed folds. We should not, however, merely dwell in them, but also live as the Fathers lived. Even these other paradises of God on earth are not without the tree of knowledge of good and evil, or the wicked guide. Instructed by the examples from former times, however, we can pay heed to the sole wise and good Counsellor, and follow in the steps of those who were, and are now, obedient to Him, imitating their conversation, to use the apostle's expression (*cf.* Heb. 13:7), as we have seen the outcome of their lives. There are also wild animals and cattle in the desert and in these hallowed sanctuaries, and we must greatly fear lest any of us should fail to imitate John's way of life, as far as is possible, and be reckoned among the senseless beasts and become like them (*cf.* Ps. 49:12, 20).

What else? John always had his head uncovered as a sign of unceasing prayer, and boldness towards God, for when a man prays he should have his head uncovered, according to the apostle (*cf.* 1 Cor. 11:4), that with unveiled face we may reflect as a mirror the glory of the Lord (*cf.* 2 Cor. 3:18). Let those who are bound up with the world cover themselves on account of these harmful things that surround them, or rather, are innate within them, and their constant impediments, since they cannot pray unceasingly as we do. We, on the other hand, who have abandoned the world in a good cause, should withdraw our thoughts from it as well, uniting our minds to Christ in psalms and hymns and spiritual songs (Eph. 5:19), and make ourselves a dwelling-place for the saving Name (*cf.* Acts 2:21, 38; 4:12; 10:43), remembering Him for whose sake we left the world. For anyone who has retired from the world and this life's concerns for His sake obviously longs for union with Him, and this is brought about by the constant remembrance of Him, which purifies the mind.

Let us cleanse the eye of our understanding by reaching up with our deeds, words and thoughts towards God. There would be nothing to drag us down if we were only to look, as far as we can, at John's way of life. He went around without a roof over his head, so let us be content with a small shelter, and may each one of us gladly accept the modest room which the superior gives us, remembering him who was homeless all his life long. He was satisfied with "locusts", the name of a type of fruit, and "wild honey" (Matt. 3:4, Mark 1:6), a plant which grows wild in the desert, the roots of which were used as food by the Fathers who dwelt there after him. So he lived on fruit and plant roots, or honey from the mountains, had only one garment, and wore a girdle of skin about his loins, thus showing symbolically that he carried about in his body the death of the passions, and also that he possessed the virtue of poverty, teaching it to us through his actions. How well off we are in everything necessary for nourishment and clothing! We have receptacles and storehouses full of grain and wine, kitchens and bakeries, and absolutely everything we need.

Let us thank God who gives us these things, and His Forerunner, for through Him we gather them in effortlessly, as if they flowed towards us from a spring. Let us accept them to His glory, rendering Him thanksgiving through our deeds. If we are content with these provisions, which are common to everyone in the monastery, we are not far removed from John's poverty and self-control. For although he was unrivalled in all respects, yet we are nourished from God's stores, just as he was fed by God. If, on the other hand, we have possessions and stocks of our own, that is something terrible which separates us from the communion of the saints. Anyone who has withdrawn from the world and has property, which he either brought with him or has acquired here, carries the world around with him and never leaves it. Even if he is on the Holy Mountain itself, dwelling in those monasteries, which are an image of the heavenly country, as far as he is concerned, he profanes the place and stops it being superior to the world. Such a person will obviously be condemned for regarding God's sanctuary as somewhere ordinary. But did John, the Lord's Baptist and Herald, leave that peaceful wilderness? He did, but he was sent by the Lord to give His people knowledge of salvation and to rebuke the disobedient, which is why he was beheaded by them on this day. It was not fitting that he should die a natural death, for dying naturally is the sentence of Adam's transgression, which was not binding upon the minister of the commandment, who had obeyed God even from his mother's womb. The saints should lay down their lives for the sake of virtue and godliness, as the Lord commanded, so a violent death for the sake of what is good is more appropriate for them. That is also why the Lord experienced such a death. It was necessary for John's death to herald the death of Christ, such that he should go before the Lord, in accordance with his father's prophecy concerning him, to give knowledge of salvation to them that sit in the darkness of hell (*cf.* Luke 1:76–77, 79), that they too might run to obtain blessed eternal life in Christ.

May we all attain to this by the intercessions of him who obtained it even from his mother's womb, proclaimed it to those on earth and those under the earth, and guided, and continues to guide, all towards it by his words, deeds and prayers to God, in Christ Himself our Lord, to whom alone belongs eternal glory. Amen.

On Saints Peter and Paul

THE COMMEMORATION of each of the saints on the appointed feastday is an occasion for town and country, citizens and their rulers to share in rejoicing, and brings great benefit to all who celebrate. "The memory of the just is praised", says the wise Solomon (Prov. 10:7 Lxx), "When the righteous is praised the people will rejoice" (*cf.* Prov. 29:2 Lxx). If a lamp is lit at night, its light shines for the service and enjoyment of everyone present. Similarly, through such commemorations, each saint's God-pleasing course, his blessed end, and the grace bestowed on him by God, because of the purity of his life, bring spiritual joy and benefit to the whole congregation, like a bright flaming torch set in our midst. When the land bears a good harvest everyone rejoices, not just the farmers (for we all benefit from the earth's produce); so the fruits which the saints bring forth for God through their virtue delight not only the Husbandman of souls, but all of us, being set before us for the common good and pleasure of our souls. During their earthly lives, all the saints are an incentive to virtue for those who hear and see them with understanding, for they are human icons of excellence, animated pillars of goodness, and living books, which teach us the way to better things. Afterwards, when they depart this life, the benefit we gain from them is kept alive for ever through the remembrance of their virtues. By commemorating their noble deeds, we offer them that praise which, on the one hand, we owe them for the good they did our ancestors, but which, on the other, is also fitting for us at the present time, on account of the help they give us now.

When we call to mind what they accomplished we add nothing to their good deeds. How could we, given that we are not even competent to depict their virtue as it really is? For the sake of the sublime rewards promised by God, they strove honourably to the limit of human nature and showed us a way of life that was equally sublime. We certainly do not augment their treasures by praising them – not at all! But we do increase their bounty to us by looking up towards them as lanterns aglow with divine light, and by understanding better and welcoming the beautifying power which comes from them.

If, as we have said, we commemorate each of the saints with hymns and appropriate songs of praise, how much more should we celebrate the memory of Peter and Paul, the supreme leaders of the pre-eminent company of the apostles? They are the fathers and guides of all Christians: apostles, martyrs, holy ascetics, priests, hierarchs, pastors and teachers. As chief shepherds and master builders of our common godliness and virtue, they tend and teach us all, like lights in the world, holding forth the word of life (Phil. 2:15–16). Their brightness excels that of the other radiantly pious and virtuous saints as the sun outshines the stars, or as the heavens, which declare the sublime glory of God (*cf.* Ps. 19:1), transcend the skies. In their order and strength they are greater than the heavens, more beautiful than the stars, and swifter than both, and as regards what lies beyond the realm of the senses, it is they who reveal things which surpass the very heavens themselves and indeed the whole universe, and who make them bright with the light "in which there is no variableness neither shadow of turning" (*cf.* Jas. 1:17). Not only do they bring people out of darkness into this wonderful light, but by enlightening them they make them light, the offspring of the perfect light, that each of them may shine like the sun (Matt. 13:43), when the author of light, the God-man and Word, appears in glory.

The appearance to us this day of both these luminaries together brightens the Church, for their meeting produces a wealth of light, not an eclipse. It is not the case that one has a higher orbit and is placed above, while the other is lower down and passes under his shadow. Nor does one rule the day, the other the night, such that one would overshadow the other if they appeared opposite each other. Light is not produced by one and received by the other in such a way that the latter's radiance would vary sometimes depending on the distance between them. Rather, both share equally in Christ, the everlasting source of eternal light, and have attained to the same height, glory and radiance. That is why the coming together of these lights signifies their solidarity and support for one another and illuminates the souls of the faithful twice over.

The first traitor, who incited the first man to desert God, saw Him who had earlier made Adam, the father of the human race, later re-creating Peter as the father of all true worshippers. He not only saw, but also heard the Creator saying to Peter: "Thou art Peter, and upon this rock I will build my church" (Matt. 16:18). Once the prince of evil found this out, being the epitome of wicked envy, he tempted Peter, the first leader of God's faithful people, as he had previously tempted Adam, the founder of the race of men. Realizing that Peter was endowed with intelligence and afire with love for Christ, he did not dare make a direct attack. Instead he came upon him from the right flank, cunningly deceiving him into being excessively eager. At the time of the saving passion, when the Lord told His disciples, "All ye shall be offended because of me this night" (Matt. 26:31), Peter disobediently contradicted Him. He also exalted himself above the others, saying that even if everyone else were offended, he would not be (Matt. 26:33). Because he had been beguiled into arrogance, he fell further than the rest, so that by humbling himself more than them he might eventually appear more radiant. Unlike Adam who was tempted, vanquished and completely brought down, Peter, having been tempted and led astray a little, overcame the tempter. How? Through his immediate condemnation of himself, his intense sorrow and repentance, and the medicine which brings forgiveness, tears. "A broken and contrite heart", it says, "O God, thou wilt not despise" (Ps. 51:17), and "Godly sorrow worketh repentance to salvation not to be repented of" (2 Cor. 7:10), and "They that sow their supplications in tears shall joyfully reap forgiveness" (*cf.* Ps. 126:5).

Anyone who looks at Peter will see that through repentance and painful grief he not only adequately healed the denial into which he had been drawn, but he also completely rooted out of his soul that passion which had made him fall behind the others. Wishing to demonstrate this to everyone, the Lord, after His passion in the flesh for our sake and His rising on the third day, used those words to Peter which we read in today's Gospel, asking him, "Simon, son of Jonah, lovest thou me more than these" (John 21:15), meaning, "more than these disciples of mine". But see how much humbler he has become. Whereas before, even without being asked, he set himself above the rest and said that even if all forsook the Lord, he would not; now, on being asked whether he loves Him more than the others do, he affirms that he loves Him, but leaves out the word "more", saying "Yea, Lord; thou knowest that I love thee" (John 21:15, 16, *cf.* 17).

What does the Lord do? Since Peter has shown that he has not lost his love for Him and has now acquired humility as well, He openly fulfils the promise made long before and tells him, "Feed my lambs" (John 21:15). When He was referring to the company of believers as a building, He promised to make Peter the foundation stone, saying, "Thou art Peter, and upon this rock I will build my church" (Matt. 16:18). On the other hand, when He was talking in terms of fishing, He made him a fisher of men with the words, "From henceforth thou shalt catch men" (Luke 5:10). But when He speaks of His disciples as sheep, He sets Peter over them as a shepherd, saying, "Feed my lambs, feed my sheep" (John 21:15–17). It is clear from this that the Lord's desire for us to be saved is so great, that He asks of those who love Him only one thing: to lead us to the pasture and fold of salvation.

Let us long to be saved, and obey those who lead us in that direction through their words and deeds. As long as each of us wishes to take the road leading to salvation, the teacher, prepared by our common Saviour, is at hand, together with the giver of salvation, who, in His overwhelming love for mankind, is more than ready without being called or beseeched. Christ asks Peter three times so that three times he can reply affirming his faith, thus healing his threefold denial with his threefold confession. Thrice Christ appoints him over His sheep and lambs, placing under him the three categories of those being saved: slaves, hirelings and sons, or, alternatively, virgins, chaste widows and those honourably married. But when Peter was asked again and again if he loved Christ, the Scripture tells us he was grieved by the repeated questioning (John 21:17), supposing that the Lord did not believe him. Knowing that he loved Christ, aware that his questioner knew him better than he knew himself, and feeling under pressure, Peter not only confessed that he loved Him, but also proclaimed that the Lord he loved was "God over all" (Rom. 9:5), by saying, "Lord, thou knowest all things; thou knowest that I love thee", because only "God who is over all" is all-knowing.

Once Peter had made this heartfelt confession, the Lord ordained him shepherd and chief pastor of His whole Church, and also promised to encompass him with such strength, that he who previously was unable even to stand being spoken to and questioned by a young girl (John 18:17), would endure unto death, even death on a cross. "Verily, verily, I say unto thee, When thou wast younger", both physically and spiritually, "thou girdest thyself", meaning, you used your own strength, "and walkest whither thou wouldest", doing what you liked and living according to your natural inclinations. "But when thou shalt be old", having reached the peak of your physical and spiritual age, "thou shalt stretch forth thy hands". With these words, Christ indicates that Peter will die on a cross, and bears witness that his crucifixion will not be involuntary. "Thou shalt stretch forth thy hands, and another shall gird thee", meaning strengthen, "and carry thee whither thou wouldest not", that is to say, out of this life (*cf.* John 21:18). Our nature is unwilling to be dissolved in death, and Peter's superhuman martyrdom also demonstrates our attitude as human beings to life. "*Strengthened by Me*", Christ tells him, "you will willingly endure all these things for my sake and bear witness to me; for the desire to do so is not natural but supernatural to human nature".

Peter was the sort of man who can be described in a few words. As for Paul, on the other hand, what tongue – or how many and what sort of tongues – can depict even to a limited extent his endurance unto death for Christ's sake? He was put to death every day, or rather he was always dead, no longer alive himself, as he tells us, but having Christ living in him (Gal. 2:20). For love of Christ he not only counted everything in the present world as dung (Phil. 3:8), but even put things to come in second place compared to the Lord. "For I am persuaded", he says, "that neither death, nor life, nor things present, nor things to come, nor height, nor depth shall be able to separate us from the love of God which is in Christ Jesus our Lord" (*cf.* Rom. 8:38–39). He had zeal for God, and was jealous over us with divine jealousy (2 Cor. 11:2). The only one to equal him in this was Peter, but hear how humble he is when he says of himself, "I am the least of the apostles, that am not meet to be called an apostle" (1 Cor. 15:9).

Given that Paul made the same confession of faith as Peter, and had the same zeal, humility and love, surely they received the same rewards from Him who measures everything with completely just scales, yardstick and plumbline. Anything else would be unreasonable. That is why the Lord told Peter, "Thou art Peter and upon this rock I will build my church" (Matt. 16:18), whereas He said to Ananias of Paul, "He is a chosen vessel unto me, to bear my name before the Gentiles and kings" (Acts 9:15). Which name? Clearly the name we have been given, the name of Christ's Church, which rests on the foundation stone of Peter. Notice that Peter and Paul are equal in prominence and glory, and both hold up the Church. Consequently the Church now bestows one and the same honour on both, and celebrates them together with equal esteem. As we consider the outcome of their lives, let us imitate how they lived, or at least how they were restored through humility and repentance, even if we cannot attain to their other great and exalted achievements, which are appropriate to great men and fitting for great men to emulate. In fact, some aspects of their lives are probably impossible for anyone to imitate. Amendment through repentance, however, is more appropriate for us than for the great, since we all sin many times every day, and unless we lay hold of salvation through continuous repentance, we have no hope of it from any other source.

Repentance is preceded by awareness of our sins, which is a strong incentive to mercy. "Have mercy upon me", said the psalmist and prophet to God, "for I acknowledge my transgressions" (Ps. 51:1, 3). Through his recognition of sin he attracted God's compassion, and through his confession and self-condemnation he obtained complete forgiveness. "I said", the psalmist tells us, "I will confess my transgressions unto the Lord; and thou forgavest the iniquity of my heart" (*cf.* Ps. 32:5), because acknowledgment of our sins is followed by condemnation of ourselves, which in turn is followed by that sorrow for our sins which Paul calls "godly sorrow" (2 Cor. 7:10). After godly sorrow confession and prayer to God with a contrite heart come naturally (Ps. 51:17), as does the promise to keep away from evil from now on. This is repentance.

This is how Manasseh escaped being punished for his sins, even though he had fallen into many great and serious transgressions, and wallowed in them for years on end (2 Chr. 33:1–20). As for David, the Lord set aside his sin because of his repentance, nor did he deprive him of his prophetic gift. When Peter resorted to repentance, he not only recovered from his fall and obtained forgiveness, but was also appointed to protect Christ's Church. As you see, Paul too was rewarded with this rôle after his conversion, once he had made progress and become more closely God's own than the others. Repentance which is true and truly from the heart persuades the penitent not to sin any more, not to mix with corrupt people, and not to gape in curiosity at evil pleasures, but to despise things present, cling to things to come, struggle against passions, seek after virtues, be self-controlled in every respect, keep vigil with prayers to God, and shun dishonest gain. It convinces him to be merciful to those who wrong him, gracious to those who ask something of him, ready with all his heart to bend down and help in any way he can, whether by words, actions or money, all who seek his assistance, that through kindness to his fellow-man he might gain God's love in return for loving his neighbour, draw the divine favour to himself, and attain to eternal mercy and God's everlasting blessing and grace.

May we all attain to this by the grace of the only-begotten Son of God, to whom belong all glory, might, honour and worship, together with His Father without beginning and the all-holy, good and life-giving Spirit, now and for ever and unto the ages of ages. Amen.

On Saint John the Evangelist and Theologian

TODAY WE CELEBRATE THE FEAST of one of Christ's chosen apostles, and extol him as the father of all those called by Christ's name, and in particular as patriarch of those "which were born, not of blood, nor of the will of the flesh, nor of the will of man, but of God" (John 1:13). As Jacob produced twelve patriarchs according to the flesh, from whom the twelve tribes of Israel came into being (Gen. 35:22–26), so spiritually Jesus gave us the twelve initiates into His mystery (Matt. 10:2–4, Mark 3:14–19, Luke 6:13–16, and Acts 1:13). When one of them wretchedly fell away (Matt. 27:5, Acts 1:16–20), the great St. Paul, upon whom Christ had looked down from heaven (*cf.* Acts 9:3), made up the number. If we do not see the same number of tribes originating from the apostles, that is nothing at all strange, for spiritual things are divided without losing their unity. In the same way, our body apparently has five senses, but our soul's perception is single, divided yet united. The twelve wells of water by which the Israelites, under Moses' leadership, encamped and quenched their thirst after travelling in the desert foreshadowed these twelve men (Exod. 15:27). For by providing spiritual water they delivered the human race, which had previously been walking through the trackless wastes of atheism, from the burning heat of mad idolatry. Similarly, the twelve stones which Joshua, son of

Nun, set up as a sign in Gilgal after the Israelites had miraculously crossed the Jordan on foot (Josh. 4:9), foreshadowed the twelve apostles, for they are an everlasting sign to us that the true Jesus held back the river of sin that was engulfing the world and allowed those who obeyed Him to pass along life's path without sin, just as in earlier days He let the Israelites cross the Jordan dry-shod.

But characteristics such as these, and the fact of being called by none other than Christ, the only-begotten Son of God, are common to all the apostles. The one whose feast we now celebrate, however, was not just called as an apostle, but also numbered among the elect; and not simply chosen out of every nation under heaven, but selected from among those chosen ones as leader of the circle of leaders, that is to say, of the other apostles, and was of equal rank with Peter and James. Together with these two he was taken aside by the Saviour, led up Mount Tabor, heard Moses and Elijah speaking to Christ, and saw by divine providence that great and extraordinary spectacle, the radiance of the light of the Son's divinity which flashed brighter than lightning in a way defying description. He heard the Father's voice referring to Christ alone, "This is my beloved Son, in whom I am well pleased; hear ye him" (Matt. 17:1–5). In this blessed fashion John was made a disciple not just of the Son but of the Father Himself.

But even this John has in common with Peter and James, Christ's foremost disciples, just as he shares his rôle of evangelist with his fellow writers of the Holy Gospel, the words of eternal life, though he far surpassed them in his eloquence and sublime theology. As for those blessings which were uniquely his, what words can adequately portray them? He alone, not only of the apostles, but of all eminent men before and after him, was called "virgin" by everyone, for it seems that he alone kept both soul and body, mind and senses, virginal throughout his life. Few people practise bodily virginity, but nearly everyone knows what it is, whereas perfect virginity of the soul means keeping the mind free from all association with evil. So this name bears witness to the fact that John was almost sinless, and that is why he came to be beloved of Christ, who alone was sinless by nature, and he alone was characterized as the disciple whom Jesus loved (John 13:23; 19:26; 20:2; 21:7, 20).

Can you find any higher words of praise than these descriptions? Among the rest of mankind not only do we fail to find greater or more excellent epithets than these, but also to find both referring to the same man. Other, greater names, however, were his as well, for he is not just the beloved virgin, but the son of the Virgin, of the Virgin Mother and Mother of God herself. What Christ was to her by nature, John became to her by grace (John 19:26–27). If he alone was allotted the same mother as Christ, he alone of all men was His brother, kinsman to the Son of God, and like Him in all respects. Christ was the beloved Son (Matt. 3:17, 17:5, Mark 1:11, 9:7, Luke 3:22, 9:35, 2 Pet. 1:17), John was the beloved disciple. Christ was in the bosom of the Father (John 1:18), John leant on Jesus' breast (John 13:23). Christ was a virgin, and by His grace, so was John. Christ was the Son of the Virgin, and so was John. "The Lord thundered from the heavens" (Ps. 18:13), and John was thunder, for he, more than the others, was called thunder and the son of thunder (*cf.* Mark 3:17), a most theological thunder which resounds to the ends of the earth declaring the divine truth that in the beginning was the Word from the Father, and the Word was with God, and was God, and in Him was life and the true light, which lights every man coming into the world, by whom in the beginning all things were made (John 1:1–5, 9).

This thunder also revealed to us the man sent as a witness to the coming of the true light (*cf.* John 1:7), made known to us the Word Himself who came down from heaven, having been made flesh for our sake, and portrayed with the utmost clarity everything He did on earth in the flesh: His works, His passion, His resurrection after the Cross, and His subsequent return to heaven, whence He had come. All these things were written down, he says, as he saw them for us, that we might be saved (*cf.* John 20:31). He also sent out a persuasive epistle to the whole Christian community, calling all to fellowship in that eternal life, which was with the Father before all ages and was manifested to us (1 John 1:1–3). As he was amongst the foremost apostles, was particularly dear to Christ, and was called the beloved disciple, he speaks to us of the chief virtue, namely love (*cf.* Gal. 5:14), saying that God Himself is love, and anyone who has love has God, and he who dwells in love dwells in God, and God dwells in him in whom love dwells (*cf.* 1 John 4:16). He shows that love's energy within us is twofold, and divides it, without destroying its unity, into love for God and love for our neighbour, teaching that these two depend on one another for their existence, and calling anyone who thinks he has one without the other a liar (1 John 4:20). The sign of our love for God, he tells us, is that we keep His word and His commandments (*cf.* John 8:31, 1 John 5:3), as the Lord Himself taught, saying, "He that loveth me will keep my commandments" (*cf.* John 14:15, 21). "This is my commandment", He said, "that ye love one another" (John 15:12), and "By this shall all men know that ye are my disciples, if ye have love one to another" (John 13:35).

Do you see how love for God is inseparable from love for each other? That is why the beloved disciple says, "If a man say, I love God, and hateth his brother, he is a liar: for he that loveth not his brother whom he hath seen, how can he love God whom he hath not seen?" (1 John 4:20). Also, "He that saith he abideth in God", through love, "ought himself also so to walk, even as he walked" (1 John 2:6). And how did He walk? He obeyed the heavenly Father, fulfilled all righteousness, bestowed benefits on mankind, healed the sick, taught those willing to listen, reproved the disobedient, endured for the sake of the obedient being spat upon by the ungrateful, being struck, mocked, scourged and finally subjected to a shameful death. He gave His life for us, and there is no greater act of love than that (*cf.* John 15:13). But we also see that His beloved disciple was His follower in deeds. For he clearly went through all the Teacher's instructions, miracles and sufferings, benefiting everyone with his words and actions, bringing people out of darkness into light, making the unworthy worthy, and himself suffering for their sake. He did not undergo just one death to bear witness to Jesus and for our good, in other words, out of love for God and men, but delivered himself to death throughout his whole life. How many times did he suffer mockery? How many times was he struck or stoned? How many times did this propagator of godliness appear before tyrants and rulers, having to give an account of himself and being condemned! He was also exiled to Patmos by Domitian, the cruellest tyrant of all, and joyfully proclaimed the teachings of the good Lord and Teacher everywhere.

Let us too, brethren, obey these teachings and live as far as we can in the way Christ and His beloved disciple lived, in submission to our fathers. "For the obedient son," it says, "will live, but the disobedient is for destruction" (*cf.* Prov. 13:1 Lxx). Nor should our obedience be only to our fathers in the flesh, but much more to our spiritual fathers, and through them, to our heavenly Father, "From whom every family in heaven and earth is named" (Eph. 3:15). For our love, submission and obedience to our spiritual fathers is offered to God, and anyone who disobeys them clashes with our fathers' God, as Christ made clear by saying, "He that heareth you heareth me; and he that despiseth you, despiseth me; and he that despiseth me despiseth him that sent me" (Luke 10:16). "Obey them, brethren, that have the rule over you, and submit yourselves: that they may not grieve over you: for that is unprofitable for you" (*cf.* Heb. 13:17), cries Paul the great preacher, and be eager to accomplish all righteousness and every good work. If something is lacking on account of our human frailty, the Lord is gracious and will make up for the deficiencies due to our weaknesses by means of His grace, accepting us as though our good works were perfect, particularly if He sees us humbled by our failures in virtue, and not conceited over our virtuous achievements.

Each of you should benefit your neighbour in all sorts of ways, by means of what you have. Are you unable to heal the sick with a miraculous word? You can still heal them with a word of encouragement. If you personally minister to someone's needs, you yourself (how amazing!) will have the Lord to serve you in the age to come, in accordance with His words. For "He shall gird himself", it says, "and make them to sit down to meat, and will come forth and serve them" (Luke 12:37). If, however, you share with him by giving him some of your own necessities, you will have a share in divine riches and Christ's kingdom, and will be fed on ambrosia and clothed in the royal garment of immortality, as if you had given clothing, drink and nourishment to Christ Himself (*cf.* Matt. 25:34–40). Perhaps you do not have words to teach and exhort people to be virtuous, the power to rebuke, to turn men away from evil and towards virtue? Become a teacher by your actions, doing good for yourself and your neighbour. This is also a means of rebuking transgressors. Let them say of you, "The very sight of him is an affliction to us, because his ways are different from ours" (*cf.* Wisd. 2:15). If they find you intolerable and direct insults at you, fabricate lying accusations and contrive terrible plots against you, stand firm. Do not turn aside or weaken and change your course, but be kind to yourself and to them, looking to the example of Christ and His beloved disciple. Taking them as your guide for walking the Lord's straight path, travel along it without turning back. "If they have persecuted me", said Christ, "they will persecute you" (John 15:20). If you act like this and endure these things, it will be clear to everyone that you have embraced divine love.

If you long to know the signs of this love within you, I will show you them, only go on tirelessly in order to find them. When you lift your mind up to God and nothing earthly attracts it, but forgetting everything, without force and free from thoughts, you joyfully delight in the remembrance of God and prayers to Him, then be aware that you have clearly apprehended love for God and share in it for as long as this converse, or rather union with God continues. Again, when you pray to the Lord with contrition and sweet pain in your heart equally for yourself and for every man, known to you or unknown, friend or foe, whether or not he has grieved you, then know that you love your neighbour from your soul. But these dispositions will not become yours unless you possess the visible works of love. For if you do not accustom yourself to giving up your own will and do your neighbour's, how can you endure the things that he brings upon you? If you do not courageously and patiently bear the difficulties caused by men, how will you progress to praying for your enemies? If instead of obeying the one who says, "Give alms of such things as ye have; and, behold, all things are clean unto you" (Luke 11:41), you withhold them, keep them in your possession, and do not use them to meet your neighbour's need, how will you shed tears for them? "Anyone who has love", said one of God's friends, "has dispersed his money. The man who says he possesses both love and money is deluded. He is either bereft of money, or bereft of love, that is to say, of God". God is love, and He declares to us, "Ye cannot serve God and mammon" (Matt. 6:24), using the word "mammon" to mean everything we have to excess: gold, or silver, or anything else. He shows us that it is impossible for anyone who keeps money to pray, "for where", He says, "your treasure is, there will your mind be also" (*cf.* Matt. 6:21), but not in prayer. The Lord also says of such men, "This people honoureth me with their lips; but their heart is far from me. But in vain they do worship me" (Matt. 15:8–9). For that reason God's beloved thunder proclaims, "Whoso hath this world's goods, and does not give to his brethren what they need, the love of God is not in him" (*cf.* 1 John 3:17). Nor can love for the world and love for God dwell in one and the same person, for love of the world is enmity towards God (Rom. 8:7, *cf.* Jas. 4:4). So John also says, "Love not the world, neither the things that are in the world" (1 John 2:15). What are these worldly things other than means of gaining money which do not benefit the soul, carnal desires, arrogant thoughts and a will set on the earth. None of these come from God, but separate those who possess them from Him, deaden the soul of anyone they conquer, and bury it in gold and silver earth, which is far worse than the earth with which we usually cover our human dust, in that when ordinary earth is put on top of our dead bodies, it shuts in the stench of them and makes it impossible for it to come out anywhere, but the more gold and silver dust is heaped on the mind of their owner, the worse they make him smell, until his stench reaches up to heaven and there turns back God's mercies and stops God watching over him.

The beloved disciple was sent by our Saviour Jesus Christ, who loved him, to teach us the whole truth (*cf.* John 16:13), raise us up from these dead works, and urge us towards works of light. He made perfectly clear that love for God and our neighbour was the culmination of these works, and capable of bringing salvation. How can we fail to love and honour him as the one who disclosed to us the truth in its entirety? So let us not, brethren, do the opposite of what he has told us. And let us not show love and faith in our speech and gestures, while disobeying him in our actions, as John himself forbade, saying, "Brethren, let us not love in word, neither in tongue; but in deed and in truth" (1 John 3:18).

If we too love and honour him who was loved by God above all, let us show our love for him in deed and in truth, becoming not just hearers of his words but also doers. Thus we shall attain to the eternal life and the kingdom that he promised, in Christ Himself, the King of the ages, to whom belong eternal glory in heaven and on earth, together with His Father without beginning and the co-eternal Spirit, now and for ever and unto the ages of ages. Amen.

On Saint Demetrius the Myrrhstreamer

"HOW PRECIOUS are thy friends unto me, O God! How great are their leaders", says David, the most inspired singer of all time (Ps. 139:17 LXX). The leaders of the company of the apostles are the chief apostles; of the list of the prophets, those referred to as having seen God; of the whole assembly of sacred teachers and holy men, those called great in accordance with the promise of the Saviour of all (Matt. 5:19); and of Christ's martyrs, obviously the Greatmartyrs. Clearly conspicuous among these, and rising above most of them in his excellence, is the one we celebrate and honour especially today, a native Thessalonian, fellow citizen, and the guardian of our city, noble wonder of the world and adornment of the Church, Demetrius the Wonderworker and Myrrhstreamer, who was great in all respects. For among martyrs he is as a great luminary among stars, holding forth the word of eternal life (Phil. 2:16), encompassed more especially by the light of the rays of the divine dawn, and outshining most of the others. Has he not also been endowed with the grace of prophecy? If, then, he has been adorned with prophetic power, is he deemed unworthy of the ministry and office of apostle and teacher? And if he was indeed honoured with these, does he lack the asceticism of holy men, or their lifelong radiance? Certainly not. Following some, equalling others, the leader of some, surpassing others to a considerable degree, he alone, or with a very few, accomplished everything. He alone contains within himself the gifts of them all as, with God's help, our homily will go on to demonstrate, and he alone is worthy to enjoy all at once the praises due to them all.

We ourselves cannot measure up to any individual within any class of saints, never mind to a whole company or category of them, so what words shall we say in an address such as this concerning a man who brought the gifts of all the saints together into one holy life according to God, and whose worth is altogether beyond our grasp? Love, however, moves me to say what I can, the occasion calls for appropriate words, and obligation forces me not to be remiss in speaking in honour of the martyr's inexpressible greatness. From beginning to end he eagerly strove, as far as human nature permitted, to demonstrate a way of life defying description, in keeping with the indescribable rewards promised by God.

Almost from childhood he was all these things at once: a solid, immovable pillar of goodness, a breathing, moving image of every virtue; the shrine of divine and human graces, representing them all; a living book telling of glory and leading us to better things. He was an unprecedented and fortunate combination of everything noble, eager for anything good to the common benefit of all. To use the words of Scripture, being a righteous man, he flourishes like the palm tree (*cf.* Ps. 92:12), he is "a green olive tree in the house of God" (Ps. 52:8), and "a tree planted by the rivers of water" of the Spirit (Ps. 1:3), except that, according to the psalmist, that tree "bringeth forth his fruit in his season", whereas for him it was, and is, always the season of blossoming and bearing fruit at the same time. Just as, according to Scripture, the leaves of that tree never wither, so his blossom and fruit, as well as his leaves, are unfailingly bestowed on those who approach with faith.

In consequence of the fact that he brought forth leaves, blossom and fruit together and, as Solomon said, "In a short time he came to the perfection of a full span of years" (*cf.* Wisd. 4:13), Demetrius is that rod of Aaron (Num. 17:8), a fine flourishing spring of piety, a much-loved flower, a wonderful and divine variety of fruit. Or rather, he is the rod and divine sceptre of Christ, the eternal High Priest and, if you like, the ever-green, godly staff of Christ whom Aaron foreshadowed. Whereas Aaron prefigured Christ, his rod, which simultaneously blossomed, produced fruit and ripened it to perfection by divine means, symbolized Demetrius, who fulfilled the rôle of Christ's good sceptre in every respect. But Demetrius was more excellent than Aaron's rod, as someone who later acquired every virtue must necessarily be far more noble and magnificent in his character, deeds and miracles than a mere symbol. Because he pours out, so to speak, an undiminishing, never-ceasing stream of graces on those who draw near, he is like a light-bearing tree, which freely gives rays of light instead of fruit, and offers those who approach their fill of everything most beautiful and divine, while retaining its own fullness, like a sun radiating all kinds of blessings, an ever-flowing fount of graces, an inexhaustible ocean of wonders, or an ineffable, unfathomable abyss of visible and invisible benefits.

To attempt to praise someone so great by referring to his external circumstances: to say that this city which bore him is the crowning glory of Thessaly, whose very name refers to its power, or to mention the renown of his forefathers or his parents' high reputation, even though these factors increase our admiration for him, would still be superfluous. For it is rather Demetrius, who is a great source of pride to his town and his forebears. How can they be a credit to him, when he himself beautifies the whole world and even the heavenly order? What, though, does he have to adorn him? Unshakable faith, grace freely bestowed, the inalienable divine wealth of godly virtues, which are stored up for him now in heaven, swelling the treasures there of beautiful things. In fact, as soon as he was born of human parents, while still in this life Demetrius reached heaven from earth, being a great addition to the sum of eternal blessings, and a source of beauty for the whole world and for heaven.

Foreseeing this, David pronounced him blessed and extolled him, saying, "Blessed is the man that walketh not in the counsel of the ungodly, nor standeth in the way of sinners" (Ps. 1:1). He never accepted an impious thought into his mind, nor embarked on any action unpleasing to God. Preserving undefiled the grace he received through baptism in Christ, his will was attuned to the law of the Lord. He was, as it were, God's book, a writing-tablet or slate engraven by God, or a panel inscribed by God's finger and set before all for the common good. According to Isaiah, "Before he knew evil, he chose the good" (Isa. 7:15 LXX), and in the very flower of his youth he embraced virginity. He was wholly given over to the acquisition of this virtue, doing everything necessary in order to be virginal in both body and soul, that he might become a citizen of heaven, and approach the bodiless powers on equal terms while still in his body. All the other virtues helped him in this struggle, especially his zeal for wisdom. As a result, having reached perfection in understanding and purity, while still young he soon had that grey hair which draws esteem. "If men have understanding", according to Solomon, "they have grey hairs enough, and an unspotted life is the true ripeness of age" (Wisd. 4:9).

He was a gentle young man, very beautiful to behold, not just with regard to the outward, visible man, but much more according to his inner, invisible self. When God, who sees into men's hearts, saw him, He was so taken by his unseen, spiritual beauty that He graciously willed to dwell in him, to become one spirit with him, and thus to make him holy in all respects. Whereas He found David as a man (*cf.* Ps. 89:20), He found Demetrius before he was eligible for manhood, still just a boy. He found him to be at heart a workman who need not be ashamed (2 Tim. 2:15), and who fulfilled His commandments. He found him a chosen vessel like Paul, to bear His name before nations and kings (Acts 9:15). He found him "a flawless mirror" (Wisd. 7:26), able to receive and reflect heavenly beauty beyond description. I also perceive these words referring in a mysterious way to him: "Behold my servant, whom I have chosen; my beloved, in whom my soul is well pleased: I will put my spirit upon him, and he shall show judgment to the Gentiles" (Matt. 12:18, *cf.* Isa. 42:1). He shall transform some of them, turning unworthy men into worthy, that he might be "as my mouth" (Jer. 15:19). Others he shall accuse and put to shame, showing them to be "fitted for destruction" (Rom. 9:22). Although these things are written about Christ, they will be freely given by Him to those who live exactly as He did.

From then on, this wise, virginal and holy Demetrius, noble and undefiled in every respect, radiant by nature, through his own efforts and by grace, became both a teacher and an apostle. What was said of Job from the land of Uz could refer to Demetrius at that time, that "there was none like him in the earth" (Job 1:8). In fact, even Job himself, of whom it is written that there was none like him among men (Job 2:3 LXX), did not resemble Demetrius, who was holy in every way.

Job, in an earlier time, had certainly been blameless, righteous and God-fearing, just as Demetrius was later shown to be. But Job could not be praised for virginity, whereas virginity marked out Demetrius as victoriously crowned from his youth, superior to human nature, and a match for the angels who surround God. And whereas Job's body was severely wounded in his fight against evil (Job 2:8, 13), Demetrius struggled with evil to the point of shedding his last drop of blood.

There is no evidence that Job was skilled with words, whereas for Demetrius this skill, combined with the Spirit's grace, was a weapon, an insuperable defence, a builder's tool, a farmer's spade and plough, a fisherman's net, and so on. At times he cultivated the Lord's vineyard, casting heavenly seed upon the earth, or writing the words of eternal life "not in tables of stone, but in fleshly tables of the heart" (2 Cor. 3:3), such hearts as were worthy of such an inscription. In the net of his words he caught Thessalonica, Attica, Achaea, or rather, the whole area he now embraces with his myrrh, his miracles and the universal abundance of his grace. Even then the world marvelled at Demetrius' divine words, and he was, as Paul says, "a sweet savour of Christ, in them that are saved, and in them that perish: to the one the savour of death unto death; and to the other the savour of life unto life" (2 Cor. 2:15–16). I cannot say, however, that the myrrh and miracles bestowed by God on the Greatmartyr's relics are sufficient reward for this fragrance. For, great and wonderful as these present gifts are, how can they be compared with the rewards already given to him by God in heaven, and those still in store? As Paul tells us, "by reason of the glory that excelleth, even that which was made glorious had no glory" (2 Cor. 3:10). The myrrh and miracles are, however, an obvious sign to everyone that while still alive Demetrius was the sweet savour of Christ and the fragrance of life for those who chose to listen.

As he cultivated men's souls in this way, or drew them into his net, in accordance with Christ's promise to Peter (Luke 5:10), his words were his means of accomplishing this husbandry and this saving catch. At other times, he constructed a temple for God out of living, truly precious stones (*cf.* 1 Pet. 2:5), using fitting words as his tool. When he made war on Christ's opponents, particularly those visible enemies of God in whom His invisible enemies were at work, words were all-important to him, bestowed, inspired, strengthened, put in order and transformed by the divine Spirit to be effective. As the Scripture says of the first martyr in the struggle, nobody was "able to resist the wisdom and the spirit" with which Demetrius spoke (*cf.* Acts 6:10).

I also consider that the military uniform, the ring on his finger and the marks of high rank, which the martyr put on when he received his commission from the Emperor at that time, were symbols of the office of teacher and leader mysteriously bestowed on the martyr by the true Emperor. Because of this, God's divine grace worked many miracles later through these tokens. It was obviously necessary for the original deceiver to be cleverly deceived, lest he should contrive an early death for the martyr, and he should be finally harvested before the fruit for the eternal storehouse had appeared, and as a result not bear much fruit. But when the master of envy saw the outcome of these symbols, unable to endure any longer, he incited the servants of error against the enemy of delusion, and, having seized the persecutor of deception, they led him before the "Emperor of treachery", that is to say, Maximian. In this way, Demetrius was stripped to run the martyr's race, he who had been full of indescribable graces since childhood, wise and righteous in every respect, a saint, apostle and virgin, completely pure and, without exaggeration, Christ's beloved disciple, child or best and closest friend. In fact, he was all these at once, because he attained to all the thoughts, words and deeds which are dear to God.

I am aware that you all wish to know the way in which he was arrested, and where and how he was sought and seized by the executioners. In the Church of the ever-virgin Mother of God there is an underground portico which is called the Refuge. By ancient custom they start the annual festival of the Greatmartyr from there, and come up here along the road singing hymns in his honour, until they reach this place and complete the celebration. When impiety held sway, because religious worship could not be held openly, the martyr loved to frequent that underground area. There he shared heavenly teaching with those present, and fearlessly conducted Christian instruction and services for those who took shelter with him, the truly calm haven of godliness, from godlessness, as if from the stormy waves. In those days the holy martyr was a refuge for all who wanted to be pious, and so the place itself was called the Refuge.

When those appointed by Maximian Herculius to track down the advocates of godliness found out about this, they stood by while the martyr was teaching the people there. Growing even more frenzied as they saw the assembled crowd attending to Demetrius' words, as if to God's voice, they moved against him as the leader and scattered the people. Once they had arrested him they led him along this boulevard and brought him to Maximian who was passing his time hereabouts, watching the murderous acts of Lyaeus with immense pleasure. Not wanting to be torn away from this enjoyment, he gave orders for the saint to be shut away in this place, where he was also to suffer his martyrdom. It is appropriate that we represent these events every year by starting the festive procession there and finishing it here, for at that time the martyr himself was dragged to the slaughter by this route for Christ's sake, being bidden to the greatest festival and delight.

The devil, the author of evil, strove to remove Demetrius as quickly as possible from among men. He could not bear him still to be on earth at all, to be seen by people, speak to them and be heard.

It was God's will, however, to show that Demetrius, soon to be His Greatmartyr, in addition to everything else, was also a prophet, and that he not only possessed the grace to be a martyr, but could also bestow that grace on others, because it was so utterly united with him in a way defying nature, that he had become a superhuman fount of grace. As there is no time to speak at length, what need I say? You know about the delay ordered by the tyrant, about Demetrius' imprisonment, and also about Nestor, the prophecy Demetrius made to him, his consequent victory against Lyaeus, and his martyrdom.

The supremely wicked serpent realized that the tyrant's postponement was becoming protracted, and he could no longer tolerate seeing Demetrius, who was already great even before the perfection of martyrdom, alive on earth. He therefore disguised himself as a scorpion and attacked the martyr, not however to beguile or lure him, as he had once deceived the woman of that first couple, our forebears, by means of the serpent, and then enticed the man through her. He knew by experience that Demetrius could not be deceived, that he was extremely brave and well practised in discerning what was for the best. So he did not attack him through the scorpion in order to deceive him, but to deal him a mortal blow, kill him quickly and rid himself of such a virtuous and powerful opponent. But the grace and power dwelling in Demetrius outstripped the devil's speed and diligence. By entreating God and making the sign of the Cross, the martyr used his hand to kill the instrument of death, and put the disguised devil to shame, destroying his work. In this manner he showed that, unless he had voluntarily submitted to affliction, he would not have suffered at all, as he was guarded and strengthened by Christ's grace and His might. Of his own accord, he was handed over, imprisoned, seized by the executioners' hands, and suffered as a wrongdoer by the action of wrongdoers, imitating the Lord who suffered for our sake.

So when the murderous spear-bearers arrived, sent by the tyrant, he received the last blow, with open arms, into his bosom, where he was to be mortally wounded. Or, more precisely, he accepted the many blows, the piercing points of the lances, which went everywhere, through his inward parts, his bones, his flesh, and both his sides, one from the outside and one from within. He doubled, or rather multiplied, the passion of the Saviour's side, filling up, as Paul says, what is lacking in the afflictions of Christ (Col. 1:24). He so desired to be killed and to shed his blood for Christ's glory, over and over again without ceasing if it were possible, that he received a fount of myrrh in his body from the one who knew his all-surpassing and extraordinary love for Him. Thus, when there was no more blood, this myrrh would thenceforth and for ever pour from his body instead of blood to the glory of Christ, whom Demetrius not only glorified during his lifetime, through his death and afterwards, but also continues to glorify, and by whom he in turn has been glorified, is glorified and will be glorified, in a divine way, both on earth and in heaven.

It occurs to me now to say of him what the divine Paul says of Christ. For the great Demetrius, too, commends his love towards us, in that, while we were yet ungodly, "in due time he died for the ungodly" (Rom. 5:6, 8), by the Lord's grace, of course, and in imitation of Him. Through his death this whole city was reconciled with God. For where are all those ungodly people, among whom were probably many of our ancestors? Where is the fear felt by pious Christians, which led to the desire for hiding-places? Where are those who raved against the faithful with a more than bestial cruelty? All these horrors have disappeared, and everything beneficial has come about, because Demetrius bore the brunt of the battle for our faith. Splendid, spacious churches, the very sight of which draws everyone towards them, stand above those hiding-places. Kings adorned with piety even more than with kingship, are present among us, and join us in applauding and praising the martyr's valiant deeds. All of us who inhabit this city publicly declare our faith, boasting of the martyrdom of the great Demetrius. For he has poured forth his love not just upon our hearts, but also upon our bodies, by means of the myrrh which he sends forth from his body for our good health. The fragrance of that myrrh expelled impiety from every part of the city, and made it a city of God, or another paradise, if not something even better: a city watered and gladdened by a river not of water but of myrrh. Myrrh, moreover, in which and from which is the grace of healing, through the Spirit, and the working of miracles. We can therefore address to the great Demetrius the words written in the Song of Songs about the soul wedded to God in incorruption: "The scent of thy garments is above all spices" (S. of S. 4:10 LXX).

The garment of the martyr's soul can be understood as his body, of which, again according to the Song, "the cheeks are like vessels of myrrh", and the fingers "like lilies dripping fragrance" (*cf.* S. of S. 5:13, 5 LXX). As for his pierced side, having been, as it were, opened up by the spears, it can no longer be like a vessel containing myrrh nor like lilies from which fragrant drops escape, but yields an ever-flowing, inexhaustible fountain. Instead of saying with the psalmist, "The river of God is full of water" (Ps. 65:9), we must say that God's spring, the martyr's body, is full of myrrh, miracles and healings, and, most amazing of all, although it pours forth torrents, it remains full. It is as though the holy martyr's soul uttered the same words when it ascended out of his body to God as that soul wedded to God in the Song, namely: "Away, O north wind; and come, thou south; blow upon my garden, that my spices may flow out" (S. of S. 4:16).

Thus he expelled and dispersed the winter of godliness, which in those days had been afflicting the city, with the breath of the spiritual north wind, and restored to us the spiritual warmth of piety, bestowed by the fair breath of that south wind, which blows behind the stern of those who choose to sail towards the dawn of the Sun of righteousness (Mal. 4:2). From that garden of virtues and graces, which is his martyred body, Demetrius granted that myrrh and healing should flow, making as many springs as the wounds made by the spearmen in his flesh. The mouths of the wolves, into whose midst, according to the gospel, the Lord had sent His disciple Demetrius (Matt. 10:16, Luke 10:3), opened up fountains where they bit, which bring great joy and many welcome benefits to Christ's flock, whereas the wolves have gradually all been changed into lambs. The gates of hell, the mouths of those tyrants who delivered those deadly sentences, have not only failed to prevail against Christ's Church (Matt. 16:18), even though it was exposed to their bites, but procured glory on earth for those who suffered, as well as heavenly and eternal glory.

Would you also like to know what is meant by the Lord's commandment in today's Gospel reading to those sent by Him into the midst of wolves: "Be ye therefore wise as serpents, and harmless as doves" (Matt. 10:16)? The snake protects itself but destroys others, having the instinct and capability for both defence and attack. The dove, by contrast, is innocent and not on its guard. The Lord, therefore, orders His disciples to be neither aggressive like snakes, nor unguarded like doves, but wisely to join caution with prudent innocence, and so to be in a position to defend their piety and virtue, while being guileless towards those who mistreat them, to the point of praying for them. In this way, a life-giving remedy will come into being, even for those slain by the spiritual serpent. Physicians take snake flesh, cleanse it of venom, mix it with certain foodstuffs, and use it to cure victims of snakebites. By the same token, anyone who, in time of trial, combines the serpent's wariness and defensiveness with the dove's innocence, not only puts himself out of reach of the snake's harm, that is to say, the devil's deception, but also heals those who have been bitten by snakes – those who have been deluded – by destroying the snake's evil, namely, sin and impiety.

The martyr is at hand, the Great Martyr Demetrius. After having finished his course, kept the faith (*cf.* 2 Tim. 4:7), and resisted to the point of shedding his blood (*cf.* Heb. 12:4) to uphold godliness, he was so far from taking revenge on those who had mistreated him, that by praying to God for them he stopped the wickedness of some of them, whereas others he transformed, with the result that nothing of that ungodliness remains in this city. Instead, the city within which and on account of which the divine martyr underwent violent death, stands firm and continues to exist, through his protection in all sorts of circumstances, his many and varied kindnesses, and his unceasing supplication to God.

To demonstrate this fact, rather than as a reward to him – for who can repay him for all that he has done for us? – we make much of his festival, seeking to be deemed worthy of his intercessions to God, and of the eternal celebrations of the citizens of heaven. May we all attain to this, by the grace and love for mankind of our Lord Jesus Christ, to whom belong glory, power, honour and worship, together with His Father without beginning and the all-holy Spirit, now and for ever and unto the ages of ages. Amen.

On All Saints

TRULY "GOD IS GLORIOUS in his saints" (Ps. 68:35 Lxx). Let us call to mind the martyrs' superhuman struggles, how in the weakness of their flesh they put to shame the evil one's strength, disregarding pain and wounds as they struggled bodily against fire, sword, all different kinds of deadly tortures, patiently resisting while their flesh was cut, their joints dislocated and their bones crushed, and keeping the confession of faith in Christ in its integrity, complete, unharmed and unshaken. As a result there were bestowed on them the incontrovertible wisdom of the Spirit and the power to work miracles. Let us consider the patience of holy men and women, how they willingly endured long periods of fasting, vigil and various other physical hardships as though they were not in the body, battling to the end against evil passions and all sorts of sin, in the invincible inner warfare against principalities, powers and spiritual wickedness (Eph. 6:12). They wore away their outer selves and made them useless, but their inner man was renewed and deified by Him from whom they also received gifts of healing and mighty works. When we think on these matters and understand that they surpass human nature, we are filled with wonder and glorify God who gave them such grace and power. For even if their intentions were good and noble, without God's strength they could not have gone beyond the bounds of their nature and driven away the bodiless enemy while clothed in their bodies.

That is why, when the psalmist and prophet declared, "God is glorious in his saints", he went on to say, "he giveth strength and power unto his people" (Ps. 68:35 LXX). Carefully consider the force of these prophetic words. Whereas God, according to the psalmist, gives all his people strength and power – for He shows no partiality (*cf.* Acts 10:34) – He is glorified only in His saints. The sun pours down its rays abundantly upon all alike, but they are visible only to those with open eyes. Those with clear-sighted, pure eyes benefit from the pure light of the sun, not those whose vision is dimmed because illness, mist or something similar has afflicted their eyes. In the same way, God richly bestows His help on all, for He is the ever-flowing, enlightening and saving fount of mercy and goodness. But not everyone takes advantage of His grace and power to practise and perfect virtue or show forth miracles, only those with a good intent, who demonstrate their love and faith towards God by good works (*cf.* Jas. 2:20–26), who turn away completely from everything base, hold fast to God's commandments and lift up the eyes of their understanding to Christ the Sun of righteousness (Mal. 4:2). He not only invisibly holds out a helping hand from above to those who struggle, but we also hear Him speaking to us and urging us on in today's Gospel. "Whosoever therefore shall confess me before men", He says, "him will I confess also before my Father which is in heaven" (Matt. 10:32).

Notice that we cannot boldly proclaim our faith in Christ and confess Him without His strength and assistance. Nor will our Lord Jesus Christ speak out on our behalf in the age to come, recommend us to the heavenly Father and make us His kin, unless we give Him reason to do so. To make this clear, He does not say, "Whosoever shall confess me before men", but "Whosoever shall make his confession *in Me*" (Matt. 10:32), that is to say, whoever is able, in Christ and with His help, to declare his faith with boldness. Likewise, again, He does not say, "I will confess him", but "I will acknowledge what is *in him*", meaning that His confession will be in respect of the good fight and patient endurance which such a person has shown in the cause of godliness. Take note, however, of what He goes on to say about those who are cowardly and betray the faith: "But whosoever shall deny me before men, him will I also deny before my Father which is in heaven" (Matt. 10:33). Here He does not say, "Whosoever shall deny *in Me*", since the person who denies God does so because he is bereft of God's help. Why has he been abandoned and forsaken by God? Because he first abandoned God by loving what is transitory and worldly more than the heavenly and everlasting good things promised by Him. In His turn, Christ will not just disown what is in him, but deny him himself, finding in him nothing at all that could be used in his defence.

Whoever loves according to God, "dwelleth in God, and God in him", as Christ's beloved theologian tells us (1 John 4:16). So he who truly loves God has God dwelling in him, and naturally confesses his faith in God. On the other hand, as he dwells in God, God too will acknowledge him. The words, "Whosoever therefore shall confess me, him will I confess also" (*cf.* Matt. 10:32), demonstrate the unbroken union between God and those who acknowledge Him, from which he who denies Him has distanced himself. These mutual exchanges between God and man are divinely just, and fairly reward like with like.

Although the prizes God gives us resemble our offerings to Him, consider the overwhelming superiority of God's recompense to those who, in Him, confessed Him. Each saint, as a servant of God, boldly acknowledged Him in this fleeting life before mortal men, though actually just for a brief period of this present age and in front of only a few. By contrast, our Lord Jesus Christ, who is God and Lord of heaven and earth, will speak openly on their behalf in that eternal, never-ending world before God the Father, surrounded by angels, archangels and all the heavenly host, and in the presence of all mankind from Adam onwards. For all will rise and appear before the judgment-seat of Christ. Then, before everyone and in the sight of all, He will proclaim, glorify and crown those who demonstrated their faith in Him to the end.

How can we attempt to tell of those extraordinary crowns and the excellence of those future rewards, which eyes like ours cannot see, nor ears hear, nor hearts understand? (*cf.* 1 Cor. 2:9, Isa. 64:4). But what about things visible to us now? Who can speak adequately of the divine glory which constantly accompanies the tombs of the saints and their relics, the holy fragrance issuing from them, the flowing myrrh, the spiritual healings, the miraculous works, and all the other saving manifestations to us from that source?

Shall I say something about the honours we offer them? For a short while, as I have mentioned, each of the saints fearlessly made a godly confession before certain rulers and kings. Now, however, kings, rulers and all their subjects sing hymns of praise, magnify, honour, glorify and venerate not just the saints themselves, but their icons, as lords, or as something higher than rulers and kings. They willingly prostrate themselves before these icons with joy, and wish to leave this devotion as their greatest legacy to their children, a blessed inheritance bringing sublime happiness. This is a sign, a proof, and, as it were, a foretaste of that indescribable future glory which the spirits of the righteous now have in heaven, and to which their bodies, having shared to the end in their godly struggles, will also attain in the age to come. To teach His holy disciples and apostles about the excellence of this glory and of the good things to come, the Lord tells them, "Verily, I say unto you, That ye which have followed me, in the regeneration when the Son of man shall sit in the throne of his glory, ye also shall sit upon twelve thrones, judging the twelve tribes of Israel" (Matt. 19:28). He then goes on to say generally to all believers, "And everyone that hath forsaken houses, or brethren, or sisters, or father, or mother, or wife, or children, or lands, for my name's sake, shall receive an hundredfold, and shall inherit everlasting life" (Matt. 19:29). "He that loveth father or mother more than me is not worthy of me" (Matt. 10:37).

As God the Father gave His beloved Son for our sake, and the only-begotten Son of God gave Himself for us, it is rightly demanded of us that we disregard the members of our family if they are an obstacle to piety and a godly way of life. Nor should I be referring only to relatives. Should the occasion demand, it is just and necessary for each one of us to give up his own soul, if he wants to gain eternal life, since the Son of God Himself laid down His life for our sake. As

He Himself says, "He that taketh not his cross, and followeth after me, is not worthy of me" (Matt. 10:38). The cross means crucifying the flesh with the affections and lusts (*cf.* Gal. 5:24).

In a time of religious peace, we take up our cross and follow Christ by putting our evil passions and desires to death through virtuous living. But when persecutions come, we must despise our own life, give up our soul for the sake of our faith, and thus take up our cross and follow the Lord, so as to inherit eternal life. "He that findeth his soul", says the Scripture, "shall lose it; and he that loseth his soul for my sake shall find it" (Matt. 10:39). What does this mean? Man is twofold: the outer man, that is, the body, and the inner man, the soul. When someone delivers up his outer self to death, he loses his soul, which becomes separated from him. Anyone who loses his soul in this way for the sake of Christ and the gospel will certainly find it again, having procured for it heavenly, eternal life. He will recover it at the resurrection in this new state, and through it his body will become as heavenly and eternal as his soul. To crucify the flesh with its passions and desires; to be ready for extreme dishonour and the greatest possible disgrace for the sake of a noble death; to lose your soul for the gospel: these are difficult, great and, it could be said, apostolic matters, only for the perfect. So the Lord goes on to say something both for the encouragement of those waging this supernatural struggle, and for the salvation of those less perfect. "He that receiveth you", that is to say, the apostles and the fathers and religious teachers after them, "receiveth me", He tells us, "and he that receiveth me receiveth him that sent me" (Matt. 10:40).

He arranges a welcome here for those who are perfect, and provides for the salvation of those souls who are not, through welcoming those who are. Do you see how great the reward is for receiving people who live godly lives and teach the truth? Anyone who welcomes them welcomes the Father and the Son. So how should we receive such people? Not just by entertaining them and making them comfortable, but by obeying them. On this subject Christ says elsewhere to His disciples, "He that despiseth you despiseth me; and he that despiseth me despiseth him that sent me" (Luke 10:16). But even the person who offers hospitality and refreshment to God's servants will receive a great reward if he does it for God's sake. For the Lord says, "He that receiveth a prophet in the name of a prophet shall receive a prophet's reward; and he that receiveth a righteous man in the name of a righteous man shall receive a righteous man's reward" (Matt. 10:41). How shall he receive the reward of a prophet or a righteous man? As the apostle says, "That our abundance may be a supply for their want, that their abundance also may be a supply to our want" (*cf.* 2 Cor. 8:14). Anyone who, for God's sake, welcomes a righteous man because he is righteous, and makes him comfortable, will reap great benefits, even if he does nothing exceptional and only gives a little. "Whosoever", He says, "shall give to drink unto one of these little ones a cup of cold water only in the name of a disciple, verily I say unto you, he shall in no wise lose his reward" (Matt. 10:42).

In these sayings and commandments the Lord is concerned not so much with the righteous and His disciples as with those offering them hospitality. If His only thought was for His disciples, He would simply have exhorted people to receive them, and would have requested that they be welcomed and refreshed, regardless of how it was done. But by adding that they should be received in the name of a prophet, a disciple or a righteous man, He shows that He is more concerned about the people who offer the welcome, directing their thoughts towards something more excellent, that they might subsequently gain a reward as well as virtue. Christ's Church honours those who truly live according to God's will even after their death, and every day of the year commemorates those saints who departed hence on that day and left this transitory life. It also sets before us the life of each one of them for our benefit, and shows us their end, whether they died in peace or finished their life as martyrs.

Now, after Pentecost, the Church gathers all the saints together and offers up a common hymn to all, partly because they are all united with one accord and are one, according to the prayer of our Lord, "Grant them", says the Lord to His Father in the Gospels, "that they all may be one; as I, Father, am in thee, and thou in me, that they also may be truly one in us" (*cf.* John 17:21). But this is not the only reason why the Church offers up one hymn to them all. It is also because during Holy Lent and the fifty days following, it strives to declare and magnify all the works of the Lord. As you know, it celebrates everything: how the world was made in the beginning by God; how Adam was banished from paradise and from God; how in times gone by God's people were called; how they too were cast out from friendship with God because they transgressed; how God's only-begotten Son bowed the heavens and came down for our sake, did extraordinary wonders for our good and taught the way of salvation, suffered and died on our behalf, was buried as man, rose again as God on the third day, ascended into heaven, whence He had earlier descended, with His flesh, and, having sat down on the right hand of the Father, sent down the All-Holy Spirit. Now that the Church of God has sung hymns of praise in honour of all these events, it adds what is lacking, and shows how many great fruits have been harvested for eternal life by the coming of our Lord and God and Saviour Jesus Christ and the power of the Holy Spirit. It commemorates all the saints together and renders praise and honour today to them all.

Let us too, brethren, give honour to God's saints. But *how* should we honour them? By imitating them and purifying ourselves "from all defilement of flesh and spirit" (2 Cor. 7:1), and hastening towards holiness through abstaining from all evils. If we keep our tongue from swearing and making false oaths, as well as from speaking nonsense and abuse, and stop our lips from uttering lies and slanders, then we offer the saints sweet praise.

If we do not cleanse ourselves in this way, each of us shall rightly hear from them those words God directed to the sinner. How can you dare to commemorate the names of the saints, to take them on your tongue and tell of their way of life, filled as it was with every virtue and purity? You, by contrast, have hated virtuous living and have driven away purity from your soul and body. "When thou sawest a thief, then thou consentedst with him, and hast been partaker with adulterers. Thou givest thy mouth to evil, and thy tongue frameth deceit. Thou sittest and speakest against thy brother; thou slanderest thine own mother's son" (Ps. 50:18–20).

Neither God nor His saints, brethren, accept hymns from such mouths. If none of us will take something we need from our own hand if it has touched dung, unless we wash it first, how will God accept the offerings of a dirty body and soul, unless we cleanse ourselves first? Sin, deceit, lies, envy, hatred, greed, treachery, shameful thoughts and words, and the polluted acts which result from them, are all much more disgusting than dung. But how can someone who has fallen into these be purified? Through repentance, confession, good works and fervent prayer to God.

When on the feasts commemorating the saints we all take a holiday from our trades and businesses, we should occupy our minds with the question of how we can distance ourselves from the sins and defilements into which each of us has fallen, and become free of them. On the other hand, if we amuse ourselves to the detriment of our souls, pay no attention and get drunk, how can we claim to be celebrating the saints, since we have made the day impure? I beg you, brethren, let us not keep the feasts like that, but let us, like the saints, present our bodies and souls as a pleasing offering to God on these days of celebration, that by the prayers of the saints we may come to share in that endless festival and joy.

May we all attain to this, by the grace and love for mankind of our Lord Jesus Christ, to whom belongs glory, with His Father without beginning and the all-holy, good and life-giving Spirit, now and for ever and unto the ages of ages. Amen.